# STAYING HAPPY

# IN AN

# UNHAPPY WORLD

By Marie Chapian
*Poetry:*

> *City Psalms*
> *Mind Things*

*Gift Books:*

> *To My Friend Books,* series of twelve Christian gift books

*Children's Books:*

> Mustard Seed Library (Creation House, 1974)
> *The Holy Spirit and Me*
> *I Learn About the Fruit of the Holy Spirit*
> *I Learn About the Gifts of the Holy Spirit*

*Bibliography:*

> *Help Me Remember . . . Help Me Forget*
>    (previously titled *The Emanciation of Robert Sadler*)
> *Of Whom the World Was Not Worthy*
> *In the Morning of My Life* (the story of singer Tom Netherton)
> *Escape From Rage* (the story of a former pool hustler and
>    drug addict)

*Christian Living:*

> *Free to Be Thin*
> *Telling Yourself the Truth* (with Dr. William Backus)
> *Fun to Be Fit*
> *Love and Be Loved*
> *There's More to Being Thin Than Being Thin*
> *Staying Happy in an Unhappy World*

# MARIE CHAPIAN

# STAYING HAPPY IN AN UNHAPPY WORLD

FLEMING H. REVELL COMPANY • PUBLISHERS
OLD TAPPAN, NEW JERSEY

Unless otherwise identified, Scripture quotations are from the King James Version of the Bible.

Scripture quotation identified AMPLIFIED is from the Amplified New Testament © The Lockman Foundation 1954–1958, and is used by permission.

Scripture quotations identified NAS are from the New American Standard Bible, © The Lockman Foundation 1960, 1962, 1963, 1968, 1971, 1972, 1973, 1975, 1977.

Poem from SELF-ESTEEM by Virginia Satir. Copyright 1975. Used with permission. Available from Celestial Arts, P.O. Box 7123, Berkeley, CA. 94707. $4.95 + $.75 for postage and handling.

Library of Congress Cataloging in Publication Data

Chapian, Marie.
    Staying happy in an unhappy world.

    Bibliography: p.
    1. Conduct of life.   2. Happiness.   I. Title.
BJ1581.2.C273   1985        248.4        84-15932
ISBN 0-8007-1217-X

*To Christa and Liza*

# CONTENTS

# FOREWORD

Several years ago I made a quality decision to go on my own personal self-discovery journey. I didn't want to lose the myriad opportunities for discovery and growth I knew were ahead if I just knew how to reach out for them. What I share in this book comes from the discoveries I have made and from a heart longing for you to make these discoveries, too.

In my life, the demands and pressures of ministry and raising a family seem impossible at times. My deepest desire has been to be a Spirit-filled, faith-filled, empowered *happy* Christian. If you've ever longed to feel happiness without an "in spite of" or an "except for," you know what I mean. I want my soul to be overtaken with the personality of Jesus so that when I say I am happy, I don't smother a tear or gulp on a problem too big to face. I believe I have found that place of happiness now. I'm not always on top of things and not always as triumphant as I'd like to be, but I've learned Staying Happy skills that I can never lose.

I've learned from many teachers in my life. I've learned from the surf pounding on the beach, from sunsets and sunrises, from rosebuds about to open, and I've learned from freezing winds, shoes with holes in them, lonely nights, and endless prayers. I've learned from people such as my mentor and friend Dr. Bill Backus who, along with his wife, Candy, showed me I was an acceptable and lovable person when I felt hopelessly worthless. Bill showed me there was a therapist waiting to emerge from somewhere in the jumble of my soul. He encouraged me to become a professional people helper and convinced me I could actually start at the bottom of the ladder and meet goals I didn't think possible. I will always be grateful for his encouragement and support as I labored through my years of school and internship.

Dr. Hans Selye taught me about collecting love and goodwill and he said people who do such things are people who don't need money as much as some other people "because much of what we might want to buy is given to us free."

My children continue to teach me that the best things in life don't cost a penny. They are my treasures. My students and patients teach me more than I teach them and, I am sure, give me far more than I give them. I watch their lives blossom and come alive with discovery, and I am rewarded beyond myself. The workers and volunteers in my office teach me daily about love and faithfulness.

Who teaches you? Can you make a list of the people and influences in your life? When I look back on my life, even though I am still relatively young, I can see how God has led every step of my journey. He's been there with me through the successes and the nonsuccesses. He's been there with you, too.

I have not always been wise or patient; I have not always been as loving as I could have been. In my book *Love and Be Loved,* I talk a little about my personal life, and I don't want to repeat myself here except to say it's not easy to suffer loss. It's not fun to hurt. I learned to recognize and deal with life's snares in my journey through the practical working of the power of the Holy Spirit. All that I know has been learned through need of Him.

In my ministry I see countless hurts in countless souls, but the peace is in the struggle, in the conquering, in the joyful knowledge that victory is ours. It's always ours, because we're His.

Maybe you feel you're really a nothing and will always be a nothing—did your parents tell you that when you were young? Does your husband or wife tell you that now? If you've been abused or mistreated in your life, this book is written specifically and especially for you. I don't offer any pie-in-the-sky solutions for pain, but I promise to share honestly and openly what I've learned through my own suffering, as well as through my work as a psychotherapist. The lives of many people who have shared honestly and openly with me are also represented in this book.

We are all victims at one time or another in our lives. We can learn from these dark, unhappy moments in time and become wiser and brighter because of them. Learning to be survivors means we stop avoiding our emotional injuries and sufferings and, no matter how painful it may be, face them. In time you will learn how to identify those things which are hurting you as easily as you can identify a sore throat or a backache. For now, we are going to take one step at a time so you will learn not only how to gain but also *keep* your Staying Happy in an Unhappy World principles.

I believe God is calling us to a higher life—richer, more productive, happier. I believe you can become happy and *stay* happy in an unhappy world.

Love,
Your friend,
Marie

# ONE
# The
# Victim

## *Who Is the Victim?*

When I was five years old, my mother came to pick me up from kindergarten one day and she took me to visit my grandmother. My grandmother was a wonderful lady and I adored her. She was fragile and elegant and educated. I don't remember her ever being well. She had arthritis and my only memory of her is seeing her sitting up in her bed with her hair combed in a neat, soft pile on top of her head, her long, thin arms at her sides. She used to read to me by the hour from her wonderful and brilliantly illustrated storybooks. Her voice was clear and light and I loved her deep, dancing green eyes. She had a warm smile and no matter when I popped into her room, she was always happy to see me.

We lived in the apartment next to hers, so I spent more time with her than I did at home. On that day when my mother came to get me, I ran into my grandmother's bedroom while my mother prepared lunch in the kitchen. I was alone when I found her lying glassy-eyed, staring at the wall. Her breakfast dishes were on the floor and there was cereal splattered on the wall. I couldn't imagine what it meant that someone could be dying. She spoke to me, her tongue thick and her voice so soft I put my face next to hers to hear. Her hands clutched mine, cold, thin, the life draining from them. I was unacquainted with death. I couldn't imagine a person going away forever. She didn't return when she went away to the hospital, a barely visible lump on the stretcher. It was days later, when they made up her bed smooth and tight, without her tiny, frail body in it, that I realized my grandma had gone away—forever.

Years later I understood the emotional impact my grandmother's death had on our family. My mother had insisted our families live in an apartment building next door to each other so she could nurse my grandmother back to health. She believed she could restore her to her former healthy and vibrant self. When my grandmother died, my mother was shattered. She was the oldest of seven children and had felt responsible for them while they were growing up, as well as to her mother and father. Her reaction to her mother's death was a mixture of grief and guilt. She just couldn't believe she had died. She told me years later how she believed she was a complete failure in caring for her mother because she couldn't keep her alive. The first phase of grief, ''I can't believe it,'' can take several months to go through, even longer. At this point in her life, my mother was a victim because she could see no escape from her pain. Feelings of loss and defeat immobilized her.

Let me tell you about some other ''victims.''

A lovely couple I once knew had an outwardly happy life until the husband's father was killed in a freak airplane crash. This once-happy couple was suddenly thrown into a morass of anguish. Anger, depression, and sorrow permeated their lives. The father had been a major character in the scenario of their marriage. The husband loved and admired his dad and wanted to emulate him in his own married life. He was a victim. Whether aware of it or not, a person becomes a victim when he behaves as the shadow of someone else. This couple finally separated and eventually divorced.

I know another couple who have a delinquent teenager. This teen-ager happens to be their firstborn child. From the very first day of this teenager's rebellious behavior, the parents called him a rebel. They treated him as a rebel. He became what they thought of him. One day the distraught mother said to me with tears in her voice, ''I don't un-derstand why this happened to us. We're nice people. Why couldn't our son be a nice person?'' That's victim talk.

A victim way of thinking is, *Everything happens to me.* This

thought is followed by *Because something tragic happened ...
must accept tragedy as a way of life.* Suffering the loss of a loved one
can make either survivors or victims out of us. My mother, in time,
became a survivor. She experienced the emotional numbness of losing her mother plus the feelings of defeat and guilt, and then as the
months wore on, realized she didn't like being miserable. Maybe she
really wasn't a failure after all, and even if she were, did she have to
suffer the rest of her days? Eventually she chose to be a survivor, not
a victim. She chose to find a better solution than self-denigration.

## The Victim and the Survivor

Do you know the difference between a victim and a survivor? The
times you experience untold unhappiness in your life may often be
due to victim consciousness, victim thinking, victim behavior. You
don't have to be a victim—you can be a survivor. Here's the difference:

| **The Victim** | **The Survivor** |
|---|---|
| Thinks because bad things have happened before, they will always happen. | Tells him/herself that when bad things happen it is not the end of the world. |
| Thinks "everything happens to me." | Knows and experiences trouble and pain but doesn't lose sight of blessings. |
| Sees no way out of problems. Expects disasters to happen to him/her. | In suffering and trial says, "I can do all things through Christ who strengthens me." |
| Is dependent upon others for his/her well-being. | |
| Feels rejected and left out. | |
| Takes no responsibility for his/her life. | |

The couple who lost the husband's father could not be called survivors. To this day they believe that life and the world around them is
filled with enemies and doom. Victims often feel this way. In fact, the

victim believes that his personal world is the worst ever; his life is the worst ever, and he is the worst person.

A victim is a person who lives in a constant state of fatigue or frustration. Life and relationships fail to produce rewards that the victim craves, because the victim is essentially a dependent person. Another person or a relationship, or a situation, or a cause, serves as the object of the victim's need for security.

A victim is typically a person who enters a relationship with another person hoping to fill a void in him or herself. The object of affection quickly becomes the very center of his or her existence. This neurotic dependency is followed by resentment for the very one or ones the victim needs. Victim thinking is dependent thinking, and when a person depends upon someone else for his well-being, he will eventually despise that person.

Is there a way out of victim thinking? What can you do when you are caught in the victim trap? If you recognize yourself in some of these victim descriptions, make note of them. Write them down. (I suggest you get a notebook and keep it handy as you read this book so you can take notes and do the necessary self-discovery assignments as we go along.)

Here's Max, a classic victim example. Max came to me for counseling after being fired from his last job, two years after his divorce. He wanted to know why such bad things happened to him. He didn't want me to know he had once been a minister. "The people walked all over me," he dolefully told me one day after confessing he once felt called to the pastorate. He went on to explain how "they" had hurt him and taken the church away from him. "You can have the ministry life, Marie. It's too much of a heartache for me! All those unappreciative people who just want to control you and run you. If you don't do things their way, they get rid of you, move you out of *their* parsonage, take *their* church from you."

"Did they take *their* wife from you?"

He stopped. I had opened an unhealed wound. "You mean Ellen?" He paused, then continued. "In a way, yes, they did. She met this other fellow, and ——"

"But she was *your* wife. Did *they* take her?"

"She never cared about me."

"Whose wife was she?"

"She was mine! *My* wife!"

"Did *they* take her from you?"

"No. *It* did."

"It? What does 'it' mean?"

"*It!* The situation! The pressure! The life I had to lead! She hated it. How could you blame her? The *ministry* broke up my marriage."

"Max, that's baloney."

He was obviously nonplussed. I could tell he wanted to leave. His eyes darted toward the clock.

"Max, do pressures and problems get solved all by themselves?"

"No . . ."

"People solve problems, don't they? Pressures are something *people*—individuals—have to deal with, right?"

"I think I understand what you're saying. It's the individual who solves his own problems," he said.

He fidgeted with his hands and then shrugged his shoulders. He wasn't accustomed to having his pat answer questioned. Now he did the questioning.

"Marie, do you think it was *my* fault my wife left me?"

I wanted him to hear what he was really saying. "Is that the fear you're afraid to face?" He wasn't listening and repeated himself.

"Do you believe her leaving me was a problem I could have prevented? Was it my fault?"

"Max, you're asking yourself to answer that question." He ignored my words and continued.

"She walked all over me, used me. She probably uses this new guy, too."

"If it's true she used you and walked on you, that's a problem. Are you afraid you didn't deal with your problems as you could or should have? Were they too big to face at the time?"

"*She* needs to deal with the problem. *She* never could. *She* couldn't face. . . ." And he was off on a new tangent. His misery was *her* fault. He wanted to convince himself *she* made him unhappy. He masked his feelings of inadequacy by playing the victim and blaming the world for bad things that happened to him.

Max is a victim. He thinks like a victim. He behaves like a victim.

He talks like a victim. He doesn't know that failure is not the end of the world, or that feeling helpless isn't a sign of uselessness, or that hurt is not unmasculine. Victims don't know that it's okay to be imperfect.

## Nobody Is a Victim All the Time

Max is deceived and cheated by his own emotions and ignorance. He tells himself his problems are all due to others or the environment. He doesn't believe he is responsible for his own choices. He suffers paranoid responses. He believes all his troubles are because *others* have used, abused, hurt, wounded, cheated, and stolen from him.

A characteristic of the victim is he or she does not realize that though things may be unpleasant or downright bad, things are also good. Blessings do exist. You can't be victimized by disaster twenty-four hours a day every day of your life without even one glimmer of relief and respite. Nobody is a victim *all* the time. You can be hurt by others, mistreated, cheated, and downright abused, but if you look truthfully at yourself, you'll see you have been a winner at times, too. Many times in your life you have been blessed and admired and pleased with yourself. You can learn to see yourself in a new light.

Let me tell you about Arlene. She and her husband, Lars, came to see me for marriage counseling. Arlene was filled with rage and when she spoke, it was through clenched teeth. She sat stiffly in her chair, her body rigid. Her anger was so intense, she had two doctors and a chiropractor prescribing medication and adjusting her spine daily. I have to admit, she was not an appealing sort of person. Her husband was a jangle of nerves. He was a bona fide workaholic and loved his job. Arlene despised him for it. She felt her life was a waste and a ruin because she had given in to her absentee husband for so many years.

Lars wanted to change. He wept tears of regret about the past and spent several weeks learning new living skills that would allow him to enjoy leisure as much as he enjoyed work. (*See* chapter 3 on the work fanatic.)

Arlene would have none of it. She refused to let him become the good guy in their relationship. She raged at the thought of his getting off so easily. He would pay for the years he "did his own thing" while she sat home in his shadow. How dare he think he could change in just a few short weeks when she had suffered all those years?

Arlene saw herself as the victim and she didn't want to let go of that role. The thought of Lars changing roles was more than she could stand. She had him in the tyrant role and that was where she wanted him to stay. She wanted the rest of the world to see him as that, too. No matter what he does, she will see him as a tyrant. He *can't* change! She won't let him. If he does change she won't allow herself to recognize it. He must stay bad in order for her to have a reason for being so unhappy with her life.

There is little that can be done to save this marriage. Without forgiveness and mercy, there's little hope of the balm and bloom of love. Arlene will go on hating, her bitterness accompanied by multiplied physical ailments. Lars will go on his way agonizing in guilt and loneliness—for a time. The difference in their lives is this: Lars *wants* to change. His unhappiness will not engulf him permanently. Arlene, on the other hand, who complained how Lars wasted so many years of her life, will go on to waste more years in bitter discontent and physical illness. Arlene will be a victim of hatefulness, jealousy, and a judgmental spirit unless she meets the Holy Spirit's words of forgiveness: "And be kind to one another, tender-hearted, forgiving each other, just as God in Christ also has forgiven you" (Ephesians 4:32 NAS).

I've never met a person lacking in forgiveness who leads a truly happy life. Even his or her pleasant moments are shadowed by bitterness and anger. Unforgiveness always hurts you more than the person or persons you are infuriated with. Disordered thinking and physical problems develop because of unforgiveness. I've stood at the deathbeds of people who have wasted precious years in bitterness and unforgiveness and experienced their moment of freedom and joy when they have finally breathed forgiveness and mercy to others. Jesus longs for us to be free of our pain and suffering. He made a way of escape for every problem we meet, even hate. No matter what heinous thing someone has done to you, freedom and happiness can be yours.

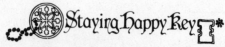

**Unforgiveness keeps you bound to your pain and makes you
a victim of the hurt you once suffered as though it happens to
you afresh daily.**

You can learn to detect "victim" thinking before it does serious damage to you as well as those around you. Unforgiveness is just one of the many warnings.

### Victim Warnings

Here are some warnings signaling that your "victim" thinking is hurting you and will only get worse if left unchecked. Below are fourteen statements. See if you can identify with any of them. Put a check by those that apply. Take your time as you go over the statements. I suggest you take at least fifteen to thirty seconds per question. If the statement only partially applies, still put a check beside it.

1. ＿＿ You usually blame someone else for your personal failure.
2. ＿＿ You are becoming increasingly cynical and critical.
3. ＿＿ You blame your staff or co-workers for all errors at work.
4. ＿＿ You are often paralyzed at the thought of taking steps toward advancement in your personal or business life.
5. ＿＿ You put off doing what you know needs to be done until the last moment, or you don't do it at all.
6. ＿＿ You make excuses for not doing the work at hand because you (a) feel it's someone else's duty or (b) you don't want someone else to benefit or get the credit.
7. ＿＿ You are disorganized at your job as well as at home.
8. ＿＿ You resent it when other people, and not you, take vacations, get promotions, or fall in love.
9. ＿＿ You feel your family is growing further and further apart.
10. ＿＿ You don't think there are many people in this world who are on your side.
11. ＿＿ You believe when people get to know you they really won't like you.

12. ___ You feel most people you come in contact with are competitive and besides that, in your opinion, they're not fair, honest, or to be trusted.
13. ___ You're physically sick or troubled with several physical maladies.
14. ___ You can see no escape from the problems in your life.

If you have checked seven or more of the above warnings, you are in a dangerous position. Your life can be flooded with anxiety and needless pain. It may be that you feel constantly threatened with some impending doom, or possibly the thought of living tomorrow with the troubles of today is just overwhelming. Read on, because there is help for you.

A victim is not necessarily a neurotic person who is constantly racked with mental agony, but he certainly does display neurotic behavior. A victim usually does not make choices to fight against trouble and danger. A victim is likely to run from danger and deliberately display patterns of weakness. The weaker we are the greater our needs and dependency. The more dependent we are, the more self-absorbed. The dependent person is only interested in fulfilling himself.

## Why Am I Unhappy?

It's important to get at the root of our unhappy behaviors. Positive or negative response to events in life are directly related to the meaning we give them. In effect, we create our own neuroses. You're upset, say, because your boyfriend just stomped out of your house without telling you where he was going or when he'd call you. You feel angry and helpless. You want to go after him, pull his arm, and demand an explanation for his behavior. "I can't handle this relationship," you despair.

Your despair may be self-inflicted and have little to do with your boyfriend's behavior. Isn't it your behavior that governs your feelings? Your words *I can't* more often than not mean *"I won't."*

"I *can't* handle this relationship" is like saying, "I *won't* do something positive and assertive to enrich this relationship." You relish being weak and helpless in your relationship. "I *can't* change anything for the better" really means "I *won't*," and you're guaranteed the right to remain helpless.

Helplessness is:

1. Honest desire to do what seems impossible.
2. Knowing that doing the impossible thing will cause hurt or fear.
3. Wanting to remember the past clearly but being afraid the memory will hurt.
4. Wishing you could discipline your child but being unable to do so out of fear of his tantrums.
5. Wanting to have a happy relationship with so-and-so but refusing to give too much of yourself because he or she may decide not to be friends and rejection hurts.

Our couple, Lars and Arlene, had to face "I can't–I won't" behavior. Lars wanted to have peace of mind but he knew that in order to do it, he would have to face his own inadequacies and that was a painful thing for him to do. Arlene wanted her husband to be the cause of her myriad problems. How painful to face the fact that *she* caused them by the meaning she attached to things. In order to be a success at her work, Arlene would have to face the truth that she still clung to her infantile dependency but accused Lars of not letting her "grow and reach her full career potential." Refusing to face her weakness helped keep her a dependent child. She was incapacitated and it was all *his* fault, she then told herself. Now she didn't know which way to turn. She had lost the ability to make wise and productive choices.

## The Hurting Self and Peace

As we have seen, the victim is dependent upon other people to blame for his or her problems and pain. A person can actually become so detached from his or her self that he stops feeling he is the actual person living his life. This is schizoid alienation and a sign of our times. Uncertainty about life itself, and our very existence, is at the core of much neurotic behavior today in that we are not taught the godly values we crave in order to feel good about ourselves. When we experience inner emptiness we try desperately to fill it. We can act out this child's sense of deprivation by trying to gain satisfaction through dependency on another person or persons. We turn our frustrations and anger inward and suffer with insatiable and unidentified longings that nobody else, no matter how dependent upon them we may be, can fulfill.

The victim is always in a state of longing. It seems as though nothing is satisfying or gratifying. Relationships based on and dictated by personal need only culminate in what Erich Fromm describes as "fusion without integrity."

The couple at the beginning of this chapter represented "fusion without integrity." When the husband's father died and was no longer there to fill the need of the family, it was as though they themselves ceased to exist. The victim has a tendency to regard loved ones as "commodities."

The victim never truly cherishes another person; he or she desperately *needs* the other person. My mother had become dependent upon her heroic cause to help my grandmother become well again. She had to come to grips with this loss and appraise herself as well as her loss. Years later, she would again be forced to face a trauma when my father was killed in a freak train accident. She, as well as my brother, sister, and I, had to discover the meaning of peace in spite of the severe pain of loss. My mother is an example of the definition of *peace*. Peace is not simply the absence of strife or trials. If peace only meant emptiness, it would be a horrible joke. Peace is not calm, nor is it necessarily quietness. It can be found in the worst cacophony. Often you will be called upon to experience peace in the middle of clamor and turmoil. If you will learn the first skill in this book, you will learn the joy of peace in the midst of trying circumstances.

**Peace is the total realization of God's intention in your life.**

In James Draper's book *Discover Joy,* he tells us the reward of knowing Jesus Christ is "grace" and "peace." We receive God's grace, which produces peace in our lives. God is the only Source of peace and well-being. The absence of problems does not give you peace. Peace comes only from walking in fellowship and being in harmony with your heavenly Father.

If you have experienced painful events and gone through some hurtful situations, you can begin to use some new methods to help you see more clearly as well as feel better emotionally.

1. Identify the situation for what it was at the time. If it was unpleasant, whether or not it was instigated by you, tell it to yourself exactly as it happened. Take your time. Try not to be led by your emotions.

2. Leave the situation right where it is. Imagine you're scooping it up in a bag and tying a heavy rope around it. Tell the Lord, "Your burden is light and Your yoke easy. Here, You take this from me . . . I don't want to think like a victim any longer."

That may have been difficult to do and you may have to come back to this exercise again. In order to be free within, you have to get rid of your victim mentality.

Stop taking your "victim mentality" with you wherever you go and whenever you encounter conflict. You become so accustomed to it that you think it's the real you and rob yourself of the good you could be experiencing.

## Making Changes That Count

Decide to change now. Here is the opportunity to become a free person, possibly for the first time in your life. When you close yourself off from facing irrational thinking, you do it for two reasons: one, you inwardly believe you or the life you lead is supposed to somehow be perfect, spotless, masterfully led, and exemplary; and two, because your life isn't this way, it must be the most horrible thing in the world. How can you face such failure? These notions are untrue. They are misbeliefs. (Read *Telling Yourself the Truth,* written by Dr. William Backus and myself, for an explanation of our coined word *misbelief.*)

Ask yourself the following:

1. Is it difficult for you to face the thought that you may be wrong or that you've failed?

2. When you don't feel good about yourself do you blame someone else or something else?

3. Can you admit you aren't all you want people to think you are?

If you do not feel good about yourself, you can learn new behavior so you will feel good about yourself. Tell yourself that from now on you are going to learn and enjoy the experience of being in charge of yourself.

Victim-type behavior is often mistaken for self-denial. The victim berates himself for attention, though never facing his fears and saying to himself, "I am afraid to face my misbelief that I am inadequate. What if it's true?" You will act oddly humble, subservient, selfless. But it's not self-denial. It's self-indulgence because it is feeding the very part of you that feels worthless. It feeds and promotes self-hate.

Say out loud now: "I will engage in self-denial out of self-respect instead of self-hate."

Self-respect can be had without arduous test-passing and an itemized list of accomplishments. Some people work at earning approval to the drastic point where they withhold approval of *themselves* until they somehow prove their worth. What proof do you need? You're God's person! For better or worse, you're His!

Do you think of people in terms of winners and losers? Do you have to believe you're a winner in order to feel good about yourself? There is nothing inherently bad about winning or losing. The value you place on winning or losing is what counts. We have to change our thinking from win-lose to grow-gain. We have to change our victim mentality to Loved Person mentality.

I like what Archibald MacLeish, author of the play *J.B.*, said when talking about his play, which is based on the biblical story of Job. He said, "We learn about love from each other. Without man's love, God does not exist as God, only as Creator, and love is the one thing no one, not even God Himself, can command. It is a free gift or it is nothing. And it is most itself, most free, when it is offered in spite of suffering, of injustice, and of death."

## Was Job a Victim?

The play *J.B.* put Job in a modern setting. Here Job is a successful businessman with a loving and happy family. One by one his children die, J.B.'s business crumbles, and he loses his health. Finally his city and much of the world are destroyed in a nuclear war.

J.B.'s comforters are a Marxist who tells him his problems are politically caused, a psychiatrist who insists there's no such thing as guilt, and a clergyman who asserts his problems are due to the sin of the human condition.

The play parallels the biblical account until the ending. Unlike Job in the Bible, J.B. and his wife experience no miracles, no rewards for suffering. Instead, J.B. and his wife decide to go on living, growing, and rebuilding what they've lost. They decide to have more children and commit themselves to a new life. MacLeish answers the problem of loss by having J.B. choose to go on living and creating something good in life. He does not hammer his fury at the world for injustice done him—he does not crusade heaven for fairness—*he takes love instead.*

Refuse to be a victim, even though it's a victim-minded world. Joe Girard, who is in the *Guinness Book of World Records* as the world's greatest car salesman, said he prayed as a thirty-five-year-old "total failure": "God, is it true what my dad said about me—that I'll never be any good? Is that what You want for me, God? Lord, if You will help me, I promise I'll try to help other people, I swear I will!"

Joe Girard changed his victim fate and mentality. He credits his prosperity to turning his life over to God when he was desperate.

"I proved to myself that it's in overcoming obstacles and learning from his mistakes that a man really finds himself and learns to get ahead," said the world-renowned Girard. He believed his trials and heartaches were for his good and quoted Romans 8:28: "All things work together for good to them that love God, to them who are the called according to his purpose."

I am thrilled when I hear of people who relinquish their victim roles and take overcoming roles instead. World-champion skier Bonnie St. John is one such person. At the 1984 Winter Olympics in Sarajevo she won one silver and two bronze medals. She is not like all world-champion skiers, however. Bonnie has only one leg.

Brad Hudiburg is another winner. He won a silver medal in the giant slalom at the 1984 Winter Olympics competition. He is an arm-

and-leg amputee. Without God he wouldn't have gotten through the ordeals of his life, he says. Brad started out as a victim, though. He lost his arm and leg in an accident riding his motorcycle while drunk. He is not a victim now. He's a survivor and a conqueror.

"I am more than a conqueror through Him who loved me" (*see* Romans 8:37). And so are you!

Pray this prayer with me:

*Father, in the name of Jesus, I give up my role as victim. I will not be victimized. I will overcome. I will love. I will face my inadequacies. I will dare to be imperfect because You are perfect and in You so am I. All things work together for good to those who love You and are called according to Your purpose! I'm loved! I love You, Lord.*

_____
(your name)

## STAYING HAPPY IN AN UNHAPPY WORLD
## EXERCISE FOR THE VICTIM

Dare to face what you've been afraid of:

1. Were *you* really to blame for the mistake you're blaming some-one for? If you can face this question, you can face doing some-thing positive about the mistake. Remember:

It is okay to **fail**
> **lose**
> **fall**
> **falter**
> **make mistakes**
> **ruin something**
> **hurt**
> **act dumb**
> **commit a wrong**

Become aware of forgiveness as well as the loving heart of God and the transforming power of the Holy Spirit who leads you into a clean, honest, wholesome, and happy life. God forgives our failures and inadequacies. Can you forgive yourself?

2. Will you take time now to *like* yourself? (Don't go on to number 3 until you really think about this.)

3. Decide that where you are now is the best place to be.

It doesn't matter how unhappy your circumstances are at this moment—tell yourself it's the best because it's yours. Decide now to stop hating what's yours. Even if it is unpleasant, bad, or painful, embrace your life and say out loud:

I'm alive and I can love it.
Not just the good moments, but every single second of my life counts.
God's thoughts toward me are loving. I choose to think like Him.
Every mistake and hurt in my life can be turned to good.

**Now memorize 2 Corinthians 10:3–5.**

# TWO

# The
# Loveaholic,

*Without you, do-ah, do-ah,*
*my life is less than mud,*
*I'm a wreck,*
*a total nothing,*
*boop-boop,*
*without you-u-u.*

Do you recognize the familiar message in these made-up lyrics? They are the "You are my total all," "You give me breath and life," and "Without you I can't go on" messages we hear every day.

My friend Lila told me about her marriage to her lawyer husband, whom she had adored. "I didn't know all those years that being in love and caring about another person was never meant to be enslavement." Many of us allow our total being and happiness to rest in the hands of other persons. Lila told me tearfully, "I think I was *addicted* to Bob . . . I mean, I needed him so desperately to assure me, to love me, to show me I was okay. I did everything for him to earn his approval. I needed him to need me. I worked two jobs for six years to put him through college and law school. I literally wore myself ragged taking care of him. . . ."

Lila hit the nail on the head when she said the word *need.* We call our feelings *love* or *submission* or *commitment,* but really, none of those words are true. We confuse love with need.

God intended for us to be whole and healthy human beings in ourselves, able to give the sweetest and best of ourselves to others without strings. *He* wants to be our identity, our strength, our all-in-all. When you put a person in that place you'll never be truly happy. A person can't fill the place in our inner selves where only God belongs.

We believe a lot of things that are not true. Some folks believe that wearing garlic around our necks wards off colds and flu. Others believe drinking warm milk and garlic will ward off anything (and *anyone*, for that matter). We've heard we can get smarter by eating fish, stronger by eating spinach, thinner by eating grapefruit, and taller by drinking all our milk. Nathan Pritikin tells us, in *The Pritikin Promise*, that the African Ashanti eat the hearts of their enemies because they believe that will give them courage. The Kansas Indians eat dog meat because they believe that will make them faithful. The Abipone of Paraguay believe eating jaguar flesh will give them speed. The Miri of Assam eat tigers to make themselves fierce.

What you believe dictates everything you do. It's important to know how to distinguish truth from error. You've heard the songs that tell us, "People who need people are the luckiest people . . ." and "As long as he needs me, I'll cling on steadfastly" or this touching thought, "I love you so much I could die." To believe that another person can fulfill our every need is believing a lie. Certain people of primitive tribes believe that eating human brains will give them wisdom and eating raw liver will produce courage. Does that make it true? We would consider these beliefs ignorant. We treat love and marriage with the same ignorance.

Writer James Thurber wrote that we are "brought up without being able to tell love from sex, Snow White, or Ever After. We think it [love] is a push button solution or instant cure for discontent and a sure road to happiness. By our sentimental ignorance we encourage marriage as a kind of tranquilizing drug."

Thurber told a moving love story, one I like. He said, "A lady of forty-seven who had been married twenty-seven years and has six children knows what love really is and described it like this: 'Love is what you've been through with somebody.' "

Some married couples insist every moment of their lives be occupied with each other. An article in the February 3, 1984 *Los Angeles Times* told of a couple in Vista, California who took ill at the same time. The article tells how Harry and Cora Walker were inseparable in their fifty years of living together. When they took ill they went to the hospital and Harry was admitted into one room with pneumonia while

strength forever to her teenage beau at her elbow. Their life together was launched and off they went into the sunset as man and wife, Rich eager to get out of his rented tux into his jeans and tee shirt so he could be "himself."

Neither Rich nor Sissy knew how to choose avenues of independent activity to develop themselves apart from each other. They hadn't formed supportive friendships or relationships to enrich their lives. Sissy mimicked what she thought a wife's role was by dramatizing her helplessness. "Take care of me" was her constant unspoken message. Sissy played the child and Rich was supposed to play the parent, but he couldn't sustain this position; after all, he was only a child himself. He was not able to trade in his jeans and tee shirt even on a part-time basis yet.

Sissy exaggerated Rich's manly abilities because she thought that was what a woman was supposed to do, and she raved continually about how wonderful he was. Rich knew he wasn't that wonderful and as time wore on felt more and more inadequate and frightened. He was afraid to admit his inadequacies because he didn't think it was manly. Sissy's constant pressures on him to be the hero-parent added to his fears and insecurities about himself as well as the world around him. Sissy's words of praise and adoration were exaggerated and false. Rather than building Rich up and giving him feelings of self-confidence, she was encouraging fear and guilt.

After the birth of their first baby, the teenage father began drinking heavily. Before the child was walking, Rich was walking the other way. He began staying out late, getting drunk on beer, and Sissy learned he was going out with other girls. Poor, unhappy, confused, and feeling betrayed, Sissy told me, "Marie, I'm only nineteen years old. I feel like I'm an old lady."

I didn't doubt that Sissy and Rich really did love each other and that somewhere in the disorder and pain of their marriage there was some hope for their future together. I felt they missed out on a most important feature of any marriage—friendship that cherishes the other person and his or her needs, goals, wants, and dreams *apart* from his or her own.

Sissy did not know she had not been the perfect, adoring wife.

"How could he do this to me when I've given him nothing but *love?*" she cried. She told me how she never took a step without first consulting Rich, how "When someone asked me how I was, I told them about Rich," how "If someone asked me a question, I'd tell them I'd ask my husband for the answer."

Rich was confused, fraught with guilt, and defensive. "Sure I love my wife," he said. "I don't know why I do the things I do. I guess I feel like she's always on my back about something."

Their actions toward one another, not dictated by love but by need, could only conclude in more heartache and sorrow if continued without help. Their dependency surpassed their own understanding. Neither of them could see how their dependency and child-parent roles were bordering on the sadomasochistic, with Rich playing the cruel hostile parent and Sissy the defenseless child. In *The Art of Loving*, Erich Fromm said of this dependency:

> *The sadistic person is as dependent on the submissive person as the latter is on the former: neither can live without the other. The difference is only that the sadistic person commands, exploits, hurts, humiliates, and that the masochistic person is commanded, exploited, hurt, humiliated. This is a considerable difference in a realistic sense; in a deeper emotional sense, the difference is not so great as that which they both have in common: fusion without integrity.*

It took time, but Sissy and Rich learned new behaviors and new attitudes. They attended one of my Love and Be Loved seminars and it was a turning point for them. They decided they did want to salvage their marriage, they did love each other, and they could change. The major and most crucial decision for them was when they held hands and prayed and both willingly put Jesus as the Head of their lives.

As the Holy Spirit filled their hearts, they could combat the hunger for and dependency on each other. They developed individually as Christians and encouraged each other's personal growth. They became happier, more fulfilled, and less frantic for each other. They learned some valuable life-changing skills and an important key:

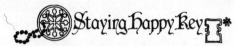

**Learn to recognize, know, and win over loveaholic tendencies before they win over you.**

## Fusion Without Integrity

Donald and Kitty are a couple who have been married for ten years. They are an example of Erich Fromm's description of "fusion without integrity." They both unhappily realized that marriage in itself did not guarantee a meaningful and fulfilling union with each other. They lived practically as strangers, although strangers might possibly be kinder to one another than they were.

By the time I met them at a Love and Be Loved seminar, they were at the point of splitting up. They told me in private that they were drinking heavily——he in bars around town and she in the kitchen at home. They fought relentlessly when they were together. Their arguments took the form of Kitty wailing and crying wretchedly and Donald screaming in frustration and rage. The underlying messages were usually the same: hers, "Why don't you love me and show me some attention?" and his, "Nobody around here cares about me and what I want."

Erich Fromm tells us that we can only achieve love when we can stand alone as singly whole and secure persons. He says, "Mature love is union under the condition of preserving one's integrity, one's individuality." Donald and Kitty wanted their sense of value and fulfillment to come from each other alone. Neither had much outside reinforcement and relief except in drinking. They constantly berated and insulted each other out of their disappointment and hurt.

## Hurt Me, I'm Yours

Kitty believed being hurt was the price she had to pay for being loved and cared for. Her father had been an angry and withdrawn man and Kitty often interpreted Donald's silences as anger. Kitty's father didn't like communication with women and felt it was demeaning and unmanly. Kitty was sure her husband must be the same and felt his moments of silence meant rejection and disapproval. Her father, after all, didn't approve of women. Kitty's unhappiness and confusion created many additional problems for her. She acted out her misery with headaches, chronic colds, back problems, and exaggerated concern for her children's welfare.

Now let's take a look at Donald's inner workings. His mother had been a busy woman with four other children to attend to besides Donald. He was stuck in the middle and grew up with a sense of frustration and hurt. He felt left out and ignored much of the time. The nonnurturing he received as a child prompted many tantrums from Donald, plus a device he used well: smoldering silences.

When Kitty became pregnant, Donald felt like the ignored middle child all over again. Kitty was like his mother, who rejected him for her new baby. He pulled the same behaviors he had as a child: tantrums, silences—but they didn't get him the results he craved. His wife was playing the child. How could she know *he* wanted to play the child? Who would be parent in this scenario? Where were the adults to save them from themselves?

Would you allow two five-year-olds to marry? Here were two people married and inflicting pain on each other, just as unattended children would do.

The difference in this case was that little children usually have an adult to protect them from each other—Donald and Kitty had no such protection. Helplessly addicted, they did not feel they could live without each other, yet they despised each other. If you make somebody need you to the point where his or her life depends upon you, he will begin to hate you. Kitty craved the love of her father when she was a child, and this craving went unfulfilled. Now she did not receive the attention and love that she craved and demanded from Donald because he was not loving her as the *child* she wanted to be loved as. Donald, in turn, was furious because Kitty would not love him as he so passionately wanted his mother to love him when he had been a child. They desperately needed to learn how to love and be loved God's way.

Donald and Kitty, like Sissy and Rich, had to start anew right from the foundation of their relationship. They had to examine their hearts and realize they were both loveaholics. If they continued with their addiction for attention and love, they would destroy themselves and each other.

## Love Me for Who I Am

Your sense of worth and being an all-right person depends upon your understanding of who you are in Christ. You will continue to act out patterns you learned as a child, as Donald and Kitty did, unless you realize that you can play an adult role in spite of the deficiencies you experienced as a child. You learned about love when you were very young, through your parents' approval or disapproval. Your parents taught you about a world in which you would learn to decide whether you are worthwhile or not. They taught you how to love as an adult through their own love or lack of it. Those early experiences, if negative, need not hold you in bondage, preventing you from ever being able to escape their influence.

Each of us carries with us an inner knowledge of our childhood. As adults we are able to make new choices in spite of our past. Many of us continue to live out our childhood as adults, and marriages cannot flourish under such circumstances.

Donald and Kitty not only accepted the fact they were loveaholics but they also began work to change. The first step they took was to discover what God had to say about them as individuals and as a married couple. They discovered the Lord cherishes us individually and that He does not see us as halves of apples needing someone else's half apple in order to be whole. There are six truths Donald and Kitty repeated out loud as they prayed for the power of the Holy Spirit to make the words live in their souls. Here are the words they copied down in their notebooks and told themselves every day:

- I am complete in Christ.
- I am a worthwhile and lovable person just as I am.
- I stand alone before God as a whole person.
- I have talents and abilities that God gives me because He expresses Himself through me.
- I am a lover, overflowing with good to give to the ones I love. My well never runs dry because the Lord is the wellspring.

- I have self-esteem and integrity of my own because *I am me* just as God intended me to be.

Walter Trobisch said in *Love Yourself,* "God's love does not allow us to remain as we are. It is more than mere acceptance. It works and forms, it carves out the image which God has intended . . . God says, 'I accept you as you are . . . but I need your cooperation—your self love.' " Trobisch quotes Martin Luther, who said, "God's love does not love that which is worthy of being loved, but it *creates* that which is worthy of being loved."

God created in Donald and Kitty new self-images, new personalities. They became new people. When that happened they allowed themselves to love and be loved.

I have a wonderful friend in Yugoslavia whom I wrote about in my book *Of Whom the World Was Not Worthy.* Her name in the book is Jozeca and hers is a love story which says, "Love me for who I am and I will love you for who you are." Jakob, her husband, tells her, "Jozeca, you are my heart," and he treats her as such. She respects and loves him as her very life. Their love story is a true one and quite inspiring. On her wedding day she prayed, "So this is how it is. I, Jozeca Podgornik becoming the bride of Jakob Kovac, Sent Man of God. Father, You have looked down upon Your servant and have blessed her beyond her imaginings. You have answered her prayers and blessed her above all other maids in Slovenia because you have chosen her to be the bride of Jakob Kovac. I will try to be worthy." Jakob said, "I am the happiest man in all the world today. My bride is God's gift to me."

Jakob and Jozeca's love story continued throughout their lives, each of them supporting and nurturing the other. They went through a war, prison, the birth of children, sickness, poverty, and still their love flourished. Jakob and Jozeca did not live in a world that enhanced their relationship. Their world was hostile and raging with war and terror all around. Jakob was also thirty-five years older than Jozeca. Their love had to stand alone, without much outside encouragement. They had to be strong and sane. Integrity was vital if they were to survive.

The cultures of the world where unstable foundations are laid by denying the value of equality (*"joint* heirs," Christ called us) deny human value. No person is a beast born to serve and labor under the lordship of another.

Too many people think the words *I do* are the same as "Serve me forever unquestioning and fulfill my every need." Men and women are equally guilty of these demands and expectations.

Men and women both demand that the force of love be kept alive by the *other* person, not themselves. There is the misconception that love is taking, not giving, or possibly, love is *mostly* taking, and a little giving.

Here's a test for you to take to see how you measure up as a lover. Are you a giver or a taker? Love takes effort and just doesn't stay alive of its own accord. You're the one who makes love live in your life. Answer each of the following questions as honestly as you can. The "loved one" in the test can be husband, wife, best friend, parent, son, or daugher—anyone you love.

### How Do You Rate as a Lover?

1. Are you friends with the person you love most in your life?
   _____

2. Are you free of jealousy and possessiveness where your loved one's interests and activities are concerned? _____

3. Do you enjoy being alone and doing your own activity while the person you love engages in another activity? _____

4. Is your loved one's work nonthreatening to you?
   _____

5. Are you secure in yourself and your own value separate from anyone else? _____

6. Have you avoided giving up your interests and becoming someone you're not in order to earn love? _____

7. Have you allowed yourself time alone for growth and spiritual renewal separate from your loved one? _____

8. Do you allow your loved one time away from you?
   _____

9.  Do you want your loved one to be happy more than you want him or her to be with you? _____
10. Are you a better person, stronger, more compassionate, giving, or outgoing because of the relationship with your loved one? _____
11. Do you feel secure in your relationship even when you are not able to control it? _____
12. Are you uncritical toward your loved one if he or she does not do or think as you want? _____

Scoring. Give yourself 2 points for every yes answer and score yourself as follows:

*24–22 points:*  You're a lover who no doubt leads an exemplary life of loving, nurturing, and caring.

*20–18 points:*  You could be in danger of hurting yourself and hurting someone else. Stop now and tell yourself: "I am a person of value. My loved one is a person of value. Neither of our thoughts or hearts are more precious than the other's. I choose to see us as *both* precious in the sight of God *now,* and I refuse to put either of us down in any way, be it by action, word, or thought.

*16 points or less:*  I know you are hurting. Go back to the six statements on page 37 and repeat them daily. Reread this chapter and tell yourself, "I *can* change." With God's help, there is hope and a new life for you, but you must accept the fact that God wants your happiness and well-being because *He* loves you.

We can love one another for who we are and we can stop demanding that others be what we neurotically think we need them to be. We can stop our insistence that our loved ones fulfill a vacant hole within our beings. We can stop demanding that this hole we have created be filled with the adoration of another. Love will not mollify the pain and loneliness any more than drugs will. Sometimes what we believe to be passionate love is only proof of our loneliness. If we enter marriage with more need than true love, we are bound to meet conflict. To paraphrase Fromm, true love says, "I want my loved one to grow and learn for his own sake, and in his own ways, and not for the purpose of serving me." Being independent and being in love is possible with the power of the Holy Spirit at the core of the relationship.

We see in Queen Esther a biblical example of the independence I'm talking about. Esther was not a nervous, shy, or passive person who craved love and attention. Suppose Esther had had very little self-confidence and, like Sissy and Kitty, preferred to think of herself as a helpless child?

Queen Esther would have been of little service to the Lord had she not been the strong and confident woman she was. She had the courage as well as the know-how to approach her husband about the dilemma her people were facing. She was no whimpering, sniveling, frustrated child-housewife. She was not hostile or vindictive and smitten with a thousand haunting rages stemming from an unfulfilled childhood. She was a woman worthy of her title: queen.

She was an orphan child, raised by her uncle Mordecai, and she was now placed in the position where she was married to the king of Persia, the most powerful man alive. Did this frighten her or intimidate her? It did not. She was prepared. She had confidence and integrity. Esther was able to communicate with the king on an equal footing.

Queen Esther, Jozeca, and Jakob show us how people can love and cherish one another equally. *Love is when a person cherishes the loved one's growth and self-discovery as much as his or her own.* Yet every day a new poem or song is written about clinging, cloying, and going mad without the object of his or her passion. Every day someone somewhere tells someone else, "I couldn't live a single minute without you."

Is it wrong to say, "I can't live a single moment without you"? The answer is no, it's not wrong because this sometimes expresses true, all-consuming feelings of deepest love, trust, and fulfillment. Once you experience love when you've been without love, your senses and expressions of affection are more than perfunctory. Your words express emotions that are vital and passionate. This is good. The danger is when the words have more depth and passion than the feelings. To cherish another person's growth as much as your own is to be unselfish. The person with the skills of love puts up blockades against self-seeking.

Love "seeketh not her own," according to 1 Corinthians 13:5. Love seeks God. Novelist Graham Greene said, "He who seeks God has already found Him." If we don't know what love is we are always and perpetually seeking ourselves, or seeking to gratify ourselves outside of God. We search and grasp at things, people, relationships, loves, but we never find "ourselves" because love isn't self-centered. The loveaholic is basically a self-centered, self-seeking person trying to find happiness through the commodity of love. But love is not a commodity, something marketable for personal enrichment.

Theologian Paul Tillich said, "The first duty of love is to listen." A Staying Happy principle is to *listen to yourself*. Listen for those important clues you give yourself. You may be saying, "Help! I want to discover me! I want to be free of my dependency behavior!" If the way seems dark, don't despair. The Holy Spirit of God causes you to plumb deeper for the depth of God's love. Corrie ten Boom said, "The love of Jesus is deeper than the deepest darkness."

## Love and Your Thoughts

"Thought constitutes man's greatness," philosopher Pascal said. What thoughts fill your mind concerning your own worth and your lovability? Epictetus, the Greek philosopher, said we ought to be more concerned about removing wrong thoughts from the mind than about removing "tumors and abscesses from the body." If you are telling yourself you are less than a whole person, you're in need of the truth. Historian Thomas Carlyle said, "It is the thought of man . . . by which man works all things whatsoever. All that he does and brings to pass is the vesture of a thought."

We look for God to answer from *without* when Christ, the hope of glory, is *within* us (Colossians 1:27). Love is known by the action it prompts, and the action is prompted by the thoughts you nurture in your mind.

What thoughts do you fill your mind with? Are they thoughts of craving, longing, and desperately needing to be cared for and loved? If so, everything you do and speak will be affected by these thoughts. You can think an untrue thought enough times until you actually believe it's true. It may be a bold-faced lie, but if you tell it to yourself often enough you'll think it's true. "Nobody loves me" spoken to yourself enough times will produce unlovely behavior and become its own self-fulfilling prophecy.

I conducted a survey while writing this book and gathered over four hundred responses from people telling me what makes them happy and unhappy. I called it a self-discovery inventory and on it I asked the question "When in your past were you the happiest?" I was surprised at the responses. Many people said nothing about being in love, but they did express *need*. Let me share some of the positive responses as well as some of the self-downing ones.

First the positive:

In the past I was happiest:

- when I was successful at my job.
- when I accomplished what I set out to do.
- when I first came to know Jesus.
- when my children were born.
- when I discovered myself as a person apart from my family.
- when with my family.
- when with my family and praising the Lord.
- when my mind has been at peace.
- raising my children.
- when the Holy Spirit has spoken to me.
- seeing my nephew accept the Lord.
- when I had a volunteer job helping people without pay.
- when I've worked hard sacrificially.
- when I've known I was important to something or someone.

Now the self-downing, negative responses:

- when I've been in love because now I'm no longer lovable.
- when my ex-boyfriend approved of me and praised me.
- can't remember.
- I am never happy.
- when somebody made me believe he/she loved me.
- when I've gotten things I've wanted.
- when I was little and people treated me special. Now that I'm big I'm not special.

One woman wrote, "I have not been happy since I have not been in love." These are words of the loveaholic. So are these words: "I was happiest when I was a child and my life was free of complexities I face now." The loveaholic is a person who does not think his or her will plays an important part in the scheme of life. Your will does play an important part, however, and just as you chose unhappy, unpleasant, and untrue thoughts and behaviors in the past, you can choose good, happy, and constructive ones for your future.

Love is not easy to keep aflame. There are a lot of problems in life to get in love's way. Life in itself is difficult, but with conscious effort on your part, you can create a love atmosphere around you that is positive and nurturing, as well as enduring.

Loving is complicated and requires a commitment from us. It takes all of our efforts and resources to create and maintain a stable, constructive relationship. On the one end of the spectrum is the hungry child with unmet demands, masquerading as an adult spouse. On the other hand is the self-sacrificing masochist who mistakenly believes his submission to mistreatment is love.

**A giant step to healthy love relationships is to face our misgivings and misunderstandings about love and to realize we are worthy of being loved and nurtured.**

Your own will can be either an enemy or a tool for happiness. Use it as a tool for happiness and begin your Staying Happy program. The exercises that follow will help you make some positive decisions toward growth and self-discovery and lead you on to new areas of staying happy in an unhappy world.

## STAYING HAPPY IN AN UNHAPPY WORLD
## EXERCISE FOR THE LOVEAHOLIC

1. Decide now to stop depending upon somebody else for your self-worth. You are worthy because God says so. Read Jeremiah 31:3.

2. Tell yourself dependency is not love. Write in your notebook those behaviors where you are dependent on someone else's approval. Write down the names of the people you cling to for a sense of self-worth.

3. Do you demand acceptance from others and become infuriated when you don't receive it? Write down those instances in your notebook.

4. Tell yourself now that you will drop those demands. You can be your own person and receive the love and acceptance you crave from a rich and fulfilling relationship with God. Give yourself two new goals as your new, independent self.

5. When gaining godly independence and autonomy be certain your actions are loving and outgoing, never vindictive, selfish, or spiteful. Plan to do and say loving things by writing them down. At the top of the page in your notebook write: "The loving things I will say to my loved one(s) today." List as many as you can but no less than three.

6. Decide not to play a helpless-child role or an overbearing-parent role in your adult love relationships. Write in your notebook those behaviors that are decidedly child behavior as well as the ones that are the overbearing parent. In writing them down, choose to end those behaviors.

7. Develop at least one new interest this month that will stimulate your personal growth and happiness, as well as give you more to share with others.

8. Make a commitment to the Lord Jesus Christ to grow spiritually and become closer to Him on a daily basis.

# THREE
# The Search for Success in an Unhappy World

Now that we've discussed the victim and the loveaholic, let's find out how you view success.

## What Is Your Definition of Success?

Joe S. was a millionaire by the age of thirty. He drove a Silver Shadow Rolls-Royce and lived the life of a successful lawyer, judge, and businessman.

Joe had just won the primary in an election race for judge in his county. He said, "I was more surprised by how little the victory meant—it left me feeling empty inside." He had success on all sides of him, or so it seemed. *It's not important whether you have money or not. It's what you do with your life that's the key,* Joe thought. He was deeply burdened and couldn't sleep. After praying, reading the Word, and soul-searching, he made his decision to become a priest.

"I'm a lot more satisfied with my life now," says Father Joseph. "I know the true feeling of happiness that comes from helping others. I'd rather wear a clerical collar than a judge's robes, and I'm happy driving my Ford LTD instead of my Rolls."

The dictionary definition of *success* is, "The favorable termination of a venture." Earl Nightingale defines success this way: "Success is the progressive realization of a worthy ideal." Denis Waitley says, in his book *Seeds of Greatness,* it's when you are working and moving toward an accomplishment that brings you respect and dignity that you are succeeding. He says, "It's not what you get that makes you successful, it's what you are continuing to do with what you've got."

Success is a process more than a realization. In the past I have defined *success* as "happiness." Possibly that definition is too simplistic because happiness can be experienced at several stages of life—not just at the conclusion of a worthy project or venture, but in the process of achieving it.

Nobody else can define *success* for you. You are the one who chooses how successful you are going to be and what success means to you. The Reverend Robert Schuller says that a secret ingredient of successful people is being tough. In his book *Tough Times Never Last but Tough People Do,* he says successful people are not more exempt from problems than anyone else. In fact, Schuller claims success creates more problems.

One problem success brings is more responsibility. The thrill of achievement fades quickly. Your definition of *success* will need to be more than achievement. Happiness does not necessarily follow success. Success in achievement may only inspire you to work harder to try to recapture the feeling you once had from being on top. Achievement drives itself to more achievement.

Low self-esteem can be a strong motivating factor in striving for success. It becomes a painful struggle to prove yourself while never feeling a true sense of "arriving" because success can so easily be lost. You lose much when your definition of *success* is based on an all-or-nothing system of self-evaluation with highly unrealistic and self-defeating requirements.

By the time John D. Rockefeller was fifty-three years old, he was a wreck of a man. He lacked humor, perspective, and joy of living. Throughout his business career he said, "I never placed my head upon the pillow at night without reminding myself that my success might be only temporary." He was the richest man in the world and yet he was miserable in every sense of the word. He was sick physically, mentally, and emotionally. But then he changed. He decided to be a giver instead of merely an accumulator. He began to give his millions away. He founded the Rockefeller Foundation, dedicated to fighting disease and ignorance around the world. He lived to be ninety-eight years old and he was a happy man in those years because of his new and revitalized definition of *success.* Without happiness there can be no real success.

The Hollywood star and strong man Mr. T. said in an interview for the *Saturday Evening Post,"* . . . My duty is to go out and spread the Word, because the Word is God. When I'm facing my Maker He's not going to ask me how many mansions I had or Rolls-Royces I bought. He'll ask me if I've fed the hungry, clothed the naked, visited the lonely, comforted the brokenhearted.'' Mr. T. is an example of a successful person because a key to his happiness is found in his words: "I'm happy in whatever situation I'm in—I could go back to the poorer days and not be unhappy.'' He is not unlike the Apostle Paul who said, "I have learned, in whatsoever state I am, therewith to be content.''

Mr. T.'s level of competence and success is evident in his dedication to helping people and investing in others and God's work.

Many successful people share Mr. T.'s philosophy and also share a life that is fulfilling and rewarding. Take fifty-seven-year-old Leo Manning, who in my definition is a successful man. Leo sometimes gets only three hours of sleep a night because he works two jobs in order to feed people who are poorer than himself. When other men his age are busy having their mid-life crises, Leo is working cleaning office buildings at night and running a cookie shop during the day. With his earnings he feeds about a hundred people, free of charge, every week. He weeps with compassion for those who come to him in need and he experiences the joy of giving—including giving up his life savings of twenty-five thousand dollars, which he used to feed the poor.

## The People Helper

Sometimes our definitions of success are beyond reality. Not all people helpers can work as hard as Leo Manning without burning out. People in the helping professions are especially prone to overdoing and becoming work fanatics while missing out on the fulfillment which sacrifice should bring. Dr. Hurbert Freudenberger tells how he was driven to help people. In the sixties, during the hippie and drug revolution, he opened a store-front clinic in the East Village of New York City, where he gave free medical help from 11:00 P.M. until after 2:00 A.M. During the day he worked from 8:00 to 6:00 at his regular practice. As he wore down, he began to lose his objectivity, something which anyone in the helping profession cannot afford to lose. He became fatigued, and almost fanatical about the clinic. He tells how he worked "like a madman twenty hours a day, neglecting my health and my family in the process." Then, typically of the burned-out person, he mourned, "What thanks do I get?" Burnout symptoms can become a positive energy force instead of a negative one. He was forced to take a hard look at himself and change. All that we do results from all that we think. This especially applies to achievement. Dr. Freudenberger *thought* he could save the world or at least the flower children of the Lower East Side. James Allen wrote, "We can remain weak and abject and miserable by refusing to lift up our thoughts." Freudenberger's thoughts, unrealistic and lofty, were low ones.

Our thoughts belong to God. Success is not a problem to Him. For the person helper who believes he or she can change the entire world, there needs to be a higher motivating force, one higher than low self-esteem and one higher than narcissism. When you see yourself as more important than you ought to be, narcissism can be the reason.

## Narcissism in Our World

Some people place achieving success above the need to love and be loved. One field of endeavor where the need to achieve can outweigh personal gratification is the sports world. Two skiers in the 1984 Olympics set the world on fire, not only by their gold and silver medal skiing but by their attitudes as well. The all-consuming passion to win was not reflected in their words before the men's slalom at Sarajevo. Steve Mahre, who was the 1982 World Giant Slalom champion, said rather flippantly, "People in the U.S. have put so much pressure on Phil and me to win medals in slalom and giant slalom; they don't realize that medals are hard to come by."

Steve's twin brother, Phil Mahre, had been a silver medalist at Lake Placid and a three-time Alpine World Cup Champion. Phil was quoted in the *Los Angeles Times:* "The Olympics aren't such a big deal. . . . You lose, so what? Life goes on." Just before the winning race and after finishing eighth in the giant slalom he said, ''I'm thinking more about the beach than the snow. It doesn't really matter, I guess.'' Hardly the psyched-up talk we're accustomed to hearing, right?

Win! Get out there and be the best! The idea we're taught is that if we are not the best, we are the worst. Being less than a winner tells us that we are less than losers. We must be the *greatest.* Before the Olympic competition began, Phil and Steve were touted by the media as potential medal winners. They were promoted on TV and their pictures were on the cover of the Olympic issue of *Time* magazine. They had won other races; surely they could win medals for the United States this year. They were the pride of the United States. Now they faced the horrors of potential defeat, as all athletes must face.

You may not be an Olympic skier but you might have pressures, whether real or imagined, to be the *best.*

The Mahres did win. The morning after their triumphant winning of the gold and silver medals for the United States, the headlines in the sports section of the *Los Angeles Times* read, ''Phil wins a gold, Steve takes a silver, but they celebrate Phil's new baby.'' Phil won an Olympic gold medal on the same day that his eight-pound, three-ounce son was born. To him the biggest event of the day was the birth of his son. Phil said, after the race, ''I came here just hoping to ski to my potential. Nothing has changed because I won the gold medal . . . the public visualizes the Olympics as an all-time high, but we race all winter long. And if I hadn't won a gold medal here, it really wouldn't have bothered me. I was never in the sport to win one, just to compete.'' Phil disproved all narcissistic jabs paid him earlier.

Twentieth-century American preacher Harry Emerson Fosdick said, ''Happiness is not mostly pleasure, it is mostly victory.'' Steve and Phil Mahre seem to employ both victory and pleasure in what they do. Phil said, ''There she [his wife] was, doing all the work while I was out there playing.'' Skiing, though the training was almost inhuman, to Steve and Phil Mahre was play. Their gold and silver medals prove their skills and sense of competition.

For most athletes, just participating in the Olympic Games is not enough. They are champions; they know it, and they are driven to prove it. The narcissist simply cannot lose. To lose would mean they are worse than nothing.

I once knew a concert pianist named Jeffrey. He was brilliant and won many awards. His talent was so dazzling that audiences and critics alike were spellbound at his performances. His years of study and daily practice were paying off. Then one day he closed his piano and refused to play again. At the crest of attaining glory, he turned his back, and never to this writing has he played another note. He won't even play "Chopsticks" for his nieces at play or "Happy Birthday" for his mother's birthday. The reason for his strange insistence never to play again? One day in rehearsal he made one too many mistakes. It terrified him and he saw it as a sign of the beginning of the end of his career. He was afraid he could not be as good as they said he was, and from that point on he'd be a flop. Jeffrey's self-worth was found in excellence *alone*. There was no room for mediocrity. To Jeffrey, a mistake was devastating.

When I was a young dancer training daily in ballet and jazz classes in New York, I heard fellow dancers cursing themselves in disgust at least a hundred times a day at some mistake in movement they made. Maybe the dreaded error was in a turn not finished smoothly, a leap that didn't quite soar right, or a wrong arm movement. It could have been that a step was forgotten or lost in a combination of steps. It was not uncommon for a dancer to curse himself loudly, hit himself on his body, and bring the entire rehearsal to a stop.

I studied with the great prima ballerina Alexandra Danilova in New York City. She led our classes with a small stick in her hand which she tapped constantly throughout the workout. She would tap our legs to correct our position as we went through our *barre* exercises. Once out on the center floor, we would follow her instructions perfectly, and so intense was our concentration that if we were the tiniest bit off in our movements, we felt somehow disgraced. The ones in the front of the class were the examples, the "favorites," the best. I was one of those "choice ones" and so I was more driven, more intense. Class never ended for me. I worked long into the night on the smallest detail of movement. A hand position, a toe pointed perfectly. I stretched and pulled and yanked and starved and sweat until I believed there was nothing in the world that could interfere with attaining the terrible goals I had set for myself as a dancer.

I had to be the *best*.

But, as Tamara McKinney, the defender of the Alpine World Cup Women's Skiing Championship, said at the 1984 Olympic Games, "So many people get tunneled on winning that they're too uptight to win. If you don't realize that there can be only one Number One and it may not always be you, then you'll be disappointed a lot."

To some people, not being the best means being the worst. In show business and the arts, not being the best can mean failure. Excellence is all-important and that is not bad, except that to some people working, studying, and doing a good job is simply not rewarding enough. Nothing satisfies the narcissist. If you don't believe what you do is special, you won't treat it or yourself as special. Your opinions of yourself will depend totally on your achievements, which you are never really satisfied with. Other people may win awards, may get famous, may star in movies or plays, may get raises, may be heralded as great pianists or skiers, and if you, the narcissist, are not one of them, you'll negate all you do, no matter how wonderful, as worthless. To the narcissist, Emily Dickinson's statement "Success is counted sweetest by those who n'er succeed" rings true. It could also read, "Success is counted unhappy by those who *do* succeed."

What happens to the achievers who have conquered narcissism? Perhaps they become like Phil Mahre, who decided to quit ski racing and said, "I'd like to settle down and get out of the hoopla." Bill Koch, a silver medalist in cross-country skiing at Innsbruck and the 1983 Nordic World Cup Champion said, "The important thing is not winning medals but striving for excellence." After finishing twenty-first in the 30K race he was quoted in the *Los Angeles Times:* "I was very elated. It wasn't a gold medal performance but I hope people can appreciate it."

## The Urge to Fail

For many people the drive toward success is accomplished by an urge to fail. Louella was a forty-nine-year-old woman who owned a small boutique. She had built up a good business and was enjoying success after two years of hard work. Then she made a major error in business judgment when she paid cash for a large delivery instead of taking the merchandise on consignment. She repeated the error and finally went bankrupt.

What was the key to her failure? Her friends couldn't figure it out because she had been doing so well after hard work, long hours, and much study and research on how to make the business prosper. Through psychotherapy, she admitted that the man she was engaged to evoked feelings of suspicion in her. She was afraid he was after her money and wanted to take over her business, or at least the profits from it. Instead of rationally breaking up with him, she unconsciously mismanaged her business so that she would not have any money. In this way she could test her loved one and see if his passion for her was real. Unfortunately, she was so fearful, she believed he failed the test. Although he had no intention of breaking up with her whether she was a success or not, her need to fail was so great that she not only destroyed her business but she also destroyed her relationship with her boyfriend and broke up with him.

Chicago bankruptcy attorney Malcolm Gaynor distinguishes between business failures which are the work of many hands and individual crashes which often involve destructive behavior. ''The same things cause tremendous success or tremendous failure,'' he said. ''Putting all your eggs in one basket. Taking a high risk. If it works, you're a genius. If it doesn't, you're a moron.''

Gaynor often encounters clients who have a will to fail. A person feels he or she is not good enough to succeed. They will unconsciously make sure they fail because they do not deserve success. Gaynor says, ''When a pillar of society steals from a bank, it doesn't make sense. He knows he'll get caught.'' He is reacting to an urge to fail.

## Success Can Be the Forecast of Failure

The achievement of success can be a prelude to failure. The achievement-oriented person is pressured to earn more money, break more records, and continually produce. According to psychiatrist Dr. Lawrence Chenoweth, the achievement of success can make a person reactive, not creative. Successful people work hard to impress bosses and treat other people as obstacles who prevent the attainment of goals. At worst they sacrifice friendships, break up marriages, lead one-dimensional lives, lack self-esteem, and become vulnerable to fantasies and psychological depression.

Many famous people have been filled with fears of success. Self-destruction often underlies the most profound accolades. Ernest Hemingway, the author who committed suicide, as had his father before him, was never satisfied with the literary achievements that had made him famous. His many other achievements in life did not bring him the satisfaction he craved, either. At the end of his life he demanded of himself that he write better, hunt better, fish better, and be an altogether better macho image. He did not regard his success or achievements as valuable.

Many famous people lack the ability for self-appreciation and self-trust. Famous and adored movie stars have destroyed themselves, unable to appreciate their own gifts or successes.

Many women fear success because they are afraid of losing their power to be loved by men. Their role as the weaker sex has erroneously been interpreted as inept. This idea promotes the attitude that success is nonfeminine. Nothing could be more ludicrous. The woman of Proverbs 31 was not inept. Male or female, the fear of success is emotionally crippling.

Here are some additional clues to inordinate success drives which may have fear of success underlying them. Psychoanalyst Dr. Edmund Bergler had a field guide for discovering when we're likely to hurt ourselves, which I've used as a basis for the following questions:

1. Do you have a contempt for moderate earnings? _____
2. Do you have high ambitions which lead you to take huge risks? _____
3. Do you have an exaggerated sense of success combined with a tendency to overwork? _____
4. Do you have a propelling drive toward more and more "success"? _____
5. Are you dissatisfied and bored when deprived of fresh business excitement and opportunities to show off? _____

6. Do you have a cynical outlook plus hypersensitivity and super-suspiciousness? _____

7. Are you contemptuous and impatient in your attitudes toward unsuccessful people? _____

8. Do you have an I-know-better attitude and are you discontent with the simple pleasures of life? _____

9. Do you have hidden doubts about yourself and your abilities to maintain your level of achievement? _____

10. Do you enjoy having a grandiose air of importance? _____

If you can answer yes to two or more questions, your drive for success may have fear at its root. Your attitudes toward success and failure are corroded with painful and confused ideas.

Fear of success usually indicates a fear that a series of successes inevitably will lead to ultimate failure. This is a gross misbelief attended by another misbelief, which is that staying in the background is a coward's way. Your drives for approval are out of proportion. You see approval as fame and/or fortune and anything less is awful. But your drives are mixed with fear and the thought that nonsuccess may be less dangerous. Not doing your best and avoiding responsibility will seem to be protection against revealing your frailties, shortcomings, and weaknesses.

What price is success? What will it cost? What will it do to your life? Will your family suffer? Will you be corrupted? You may be so afraid of success that everything you try to accomplish seems to go kaput. Fear of winning and fear of success can only mean that life becomes more and more difficult. If you are afraid of maintaining or achieving a level of success, you will set yourself up to destroy it sooner or later.

## STAYING HAPPY IN AN UNHAPPY WORLD
## EXERCISE FOR BECOMING
## A SUCCESSFUL PERSON

1. Why do you want to be a success?

2. Ask yourself if you truly enjoy responsibility. How much is too much for you?

3. Imagine the additional work, pressures, and demands that will be on you after you attain the success you desire. Take time to envision yourself overworked and stressed. What will you do that is different to avoid this?

4. Find at least three Bible verses that support your godly right to be a success in your field, and three more verses that support your right to be happily and peaceably successful.

# FOUR

# Why Do We Work So Hard to Be Happy?

Are happiness and success compatible, or are they mutually exclusive?

I sat at lunch with the president of a large, multimillion-dollar company recently. I asked him what his definition of *success* was. "Success is happiness," he answered without a pause. "I'm not impressed with symbols," he told me. "Many times our titles become our symbols and we live in them, defining ourselves in terms of the symbolism of the job."

Symbols or job titles did not impress my friend. Did money impress him? "Money is important," he answered, "but it has to be looked at in perspective. I tell my sons to work toward doing a good job, not toward something illusive like success. If we do the very best we can someone will notice us. A person doing a good job won't go unnoticed. I tell them the way to the top is never by climbing someone else's back."

"That's all fine and good for you to say," I told him, "but how about the person who is not the president of his company and who does not make the salary you command? What do you tell the bus driver who has reached the top level of pay on his job? He's never going to make as much money as you make."

"I didn't start working in this company with the idea of becoming its president. I was quite happy when I was further down the ladder. Now that I'm at the very top of the ladder I find that I am still a happy person. I don't believe that happiness has to do with your position or with money."

Did he ever worry about losing his job? Did he worry someone else might be better qualified? Did he worry about making mistakes that could cost millions? Did he lose sleep over the responsibility of a company that had always been number one? Did he worry about the company's competition? These were the questions I sought answers for. My friend answered me this way: "Oh, sure, I worry. But it doesn't help me do my job any better. I have to concentrate on what *works*, not on what doesn't. Besides, my job and the company aren't the most important things in my life."

No wonder he's a success.

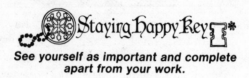

**See yourself as important and complete apart from your work.**

## The Work You Do

In the self-discovery survey I conducted, 30 percent of the four hundred respondents reported they were in work situations they didn't particularly like but that paid good money, so they stayed.

"I'm trapped in a situation I can't get out of," was admitted by people in a variety of jobs, including secretary, housewife, sales vice-president, staff clerk, and waitress, to name only a few.

It is important to think about the reason we work. In a survey conducted by *Psychology Today* magazine, out of 188,000 college freshmen, only one tenth of 1 percent of the women wanted to become full-time homemakers. Twelve percent indicated they wanted to be engineers and 10.5 percent wanted to be business executives.

Richard Nelson wrote in his book *What Color Is Your Parachute?* of a special Labor Force report by the U.S. Department of Labor. It showed that in a typical month in 1976, 4.2 percent of all employed workers, or nearly one out of every twenty, went looking for another job during the month. In actual numbers, that represented 3,260,000 people job hunting while actually employed. These figures tell us there are a lot of people who have jobs they aren't satisfied with.

Why do we do the work we do? Why do we stay in the work we

do? If money and prestige were our motivators we would probably be a world of doctors and lawyers and big corporation heads. Everyone is going to be faced with the matter of work at some time or another in life. Nineteen million new jobs were created in the United States during the seventies. Five percent of these jobs were in manufacturing and 11 percent in the goods-producing sector as a whole. Almost 90 percent, then—17 million new jobs—were not in the goods-producing sector. David Birch, spokesman for the Massachusetts Institute of Technology, says, ''We are working ourselves out of the manufacturing business and into the thinking business.'' (Quoted by John Naisbitt in *Megatrends*.)

In 1960 there were 250,000 lawyers in the United States. By 1987 the total will reach 750,000, according to the American Bar Association. The ABA says there will be a million lawyers in the United States by the mid-1990s. We are fast becoming an information society rather than an industrial one. We are literacy-intensive but our education system is becoming increasingly inferior. We are entering a new information age and it is vital that you and I see where we belong in it and what our wants are if we want to be in charge of our own world. A secret of staying happy is to recognize and accept change and progress around you.

## Define Your Wants

Please take ten minutes now to answer the following question: *How many lifelong wants and desires of yours can you name?*

Don't worry about answering correctly because there are no correct answers—there are only honest ones. Use a journal or notebook for your Staying Happy notes, and at the end of ten minutes, finish your list. Make the list as lengthy as you can, going back to the dreams you had for your life as a child as well as the most recent ones you had as an adult.

A want or desire is different from a goal. A goal has a time limit and an accomplishment factor. If, say, you vow to read ten books by August—that's a goal. But if you say you want to start reading more, that's a desire or a want. Recognize the difference.

After you have made your list, review it and then answer this question: *How long have you had these wants?*

If you have fulfilled the want, put a check to the right of it. If you want to turn the dream into a goal to be accomplished in six months, place a star after the goal. If you want to accomplish the goal in five years, place a 5 next to it.

Next, rank the goals in order of their current importance to you. Now looking at the wants you have chosen, write the most important one down.

I want: _____
                              (fill in the blank)

What do these wants say to you? Why have they remained only wants and not become goals to achieve?

Thomas Jefferson said, "I am a great believer in luck, and the harder I work the more I have of it." What are your wants? Keep them before you. It's not luck that will fulfill them for you. Differentiate your wants from your daydreaming and decide if they're important enough to become goals you will make concrete plans to accomplish. Work fanatics are usually goal-oriented. They identify not only with the goals, the challenge of work, but also with the work itself.

## When Our Work Is Our Identity

The work fanatic sees him/herself *as* the work he does. The work or job is his complete identity.

Some people cannot escape what they do for a living. Jim Brown may be good old Jim down at the racquetball court, but *Dr.* Jim Brown presents a different picture. When he's introduced, he is introduced as Doctor. A schoolteacher is not introduced as Schoolteacher Smith, but Jim Brown is introduced as Doctor Brown. A minister is always Reverend. A rabbi is always Rabbi. A title becomes the person and the two become inseparable.

A man without such a prefix to his name recently told me how he could not separate his work from himself. He said, "My work and I are one, Marie. I can't think of myself in any way whole outside of my work. I mean, work is *life.*" He was his own "symbol." When he went on vacation he combined vacation and work. He took clients fishing; he went golfing with account managers; if he went hunting, it was with prospective buyers. His lunches in elegant restaurants were for business purposes only. A year ago when he took his wife to Tahiti, he spent the whole time negotiating a deal with another account executive. He was not only a husband, father, churchgoer, nice guy—he was, first and foremost, his job.

And not for the money. Money was a secondary reinforcer. What could he buy? He had everything he needed, he said.

Ann is vice-president of marketing for a chain of department stores. Her salary is low compared to the hours she puts in on the job. She works well over eighty hours a week and recently rented an apartment in Manhattan close to the New York office, so on those late nights working into the wee hours she does not have to commute back to her home in New Jersey. The move was expensive and it took every penny she had to get the deposit together, but Ann doesn't care about money. She loves the *job*—and she loves the title. She is one of the first women to hold down a position that is usually held by men. Not only is Ann motivated by her own desire to succeed but she also is driven by the demands of her environment telling her she *must* succeed because she is a woman. Ann is a work fanatic and she uses all the familiar excuses to remain one. The sad thing is, Ann's personal life is lonely and bereft, and she works all the harder to avoid facing personal emptiness.

A common misunderstanding about work is that hard work always pays off in the end. People like Ann, who are successful at their jobs, do not exemplify the results of all earnest and hardworking efforts. Many people work feverishly and receive little or no recompense. Or how about the person who has thrust his life into a project which fails? Many hardworking people have met with failure.

I received this note in the mail from a distressed woman I'll call Marge:

> *Marie, I am freaking out. I am mad at God. I screamed at Him the other night like I was a crazed animal. What's to become of me? Why doesn't God answer my prayers?*
>
> *I've been good. I've been honest. I've never cheated on my taxes. I'm always on time. I'm reliable. I lead an honest life—but what has it gotten me? What has my hard work gotten me? I've worked all my life, and where's the payoff?*

*Everyone else is getting the goodies. I am lonely, miserable, and getting older every day, and why? I faithfully do my work and live my clean little life as I have been taught to do, and I'm so empty. I want so badly to be happy, to laugh, and enjoy my life, but I feel alone and cut off from reality.*

I feel cut off from God.

Marge was suffering from fatigue brought on by hard work and devotion which failed to bring her rewards. She expected to be rewarded for being good and for working hard. The rewards she expected weren't there and she was devastated. The Bible tells us not to weary in well-doing, but Marge figured there was a time limit on that advice. Marge is a work fanatic. She believes she is unhappy because God hasn't come through for her. She believes that if we are good people we will have good things happen to us. In this way she can excuse her lack of careful planning and neglecting to make important changes.

We put limits on God in many ways. Marge learned later, when she became ill and had to be hospitalized, that God's time schedule was different from hers. She decided to stop ordering God around and to start accepting some of the blessings she had avoided for so long. She began telling herself the things God had done for her, the joys she had experienced, and the answered prayers she had received in the past. She chose to end her disappointment with God and to start accepting His decisions and start loving Him on His terms.

Disappointment at not receiving answers to prayer when and how we want is difficult to avoid. We think we have to somehow encourage God and do something radical to impress the urgency of our request to Him. We don't have to bribe or beg God. He answers freely. We do not have to earn His favor; we need only to *trust* Him, realizing that without Him our own strength and our own abilities are virtually worthless.

We work and we pray and we trust that God will reward us and honor His Word, which tells us, ''To obey is better than sacrifice'' (1 Samuel 15:22). We obey Him by trusting Him and praising Him. Then when an enemy called Time sneaks in, we won't lose heart. It's difficult for the work fanatic to find time to praise the Lord.

The work fanatic doesn't know the wonderful inner peace in "Let every thing that hath breath praise the Lord" (Psalms 150:6). Since everything that has breath is commanded to praise the Lord, the only scriptural excuse for not praising Him is to be out of breath.

When I was in Africa in 1980 as part of the Roger Vann evangelistic team, I was astounded at the praise and worship of the Christians there. They praised and praised by the hour! I compared the short fifteen-minute praise time in most of our church services back home to this monumental and overpowering praise experience. (Read my book *Escape From Rage* for details of this experience.) It was mind-boggling. It outstripped reason and pretense. The Christians sang— no, *shouted*—the glorious songs of worship, repeating them again and again. Instruments of all kinds played in the heat and on and on we praised, voices swelling and crescendoing beyond our mortal selves. Here in this Third World nation, sweltering in oppressive heat and poverty, thousands of believers gathered to praise the living God and His Son, Jesus Christ. I'll never forget their voices.

No amount of striving to achieve could take the place of the glory of praising God. In our work, no matter what job we hold, if we stop praising God, we lose sight of our true selves. God gives us His plan for success and our plans must be infused with His mind and heart, or we'll insist He do things our way instead of the other way around. We'll hold to erroneous ideas about hard work and success.

## Hard Work and a Plan

We often hear testimonies of how hard work brought success. It simply is not true that hard work *in itself* brings the rewards we dream of. Al, who owns a chain of fried-chicken restaurants worth 200 million dollars, has this to say about his success: "I owe it all to sixteen-hour workdays, working two and even three jobs at a time, self-confidence, taking calculated risks, setting a goal and pursuing it, saving money to be ready when opportunity came my way, and learning something new every day about the business I was in." Does this tell us that anybody can do what Al did and be the success he is? Hardly.

Notice that the long workdays Al mentions are a small part of his strategy. I have talked to many successful businessmen as well as famous Christian leaders while writing this book. One thing I have noticed that they all have in common is a solid awareness of goals and time organization. Al, the chicken magnate, would never have built his business into the empire he now has—four hundred outlets and two thousand five hundred employees in thirty-six states and several foreign countries—if he had simply worked sixteen hours a day frying chicken. That kind of hard work would not have built his business. He needed more. He needed goals, self-confidence, a plan, the ability to persevere, and lots of help. Incompetence had no room in Al's climb up the success ladder. No matter how lofty your ambitions may be, hard work won't take the place of competence.

## Work as a Weapon Against Incompetence

In the book *The Peter Principle,* Lawrence J. Peter and Raymond Hall say that ". . . in a hierarchy every employee tends to rise to his level of incompetence," which means people get promoted to levels of success too difficult to handle. Someone starting out in a position of competence in a job that he can do satisfactorily receives a promotion and is suddenly in a place of incompetence. Success is like Final Placement. The aphorism "Nothing succeeds like success" may not be true for all of us. Instead, it may be true that "nothing fails like success." Being promoted to a higher position can often mean moving into a level of incompetence, even though the promotion may be your greatest desire and goal.

Such was the case with a man I'll call Randy. Randy was hired as a worker in the mail room for a large printing company. Randy is a likable fellow, punctual, reliable, and he did his job well. It wasn't long before he was promoted and given a raise. Randy continued to do his job with minimal problems. The conflicts which arose between workers or between management and the workers were not upsetting to Randy. The work pressure was not too demanding for him to handle and he found challenge and enjoyment in his work. But then Randy was promoted again, this time to a management position. It was at this point that Randy's personality changed. He went from likable and easygoing to a nervous, uptight person. He continued to work hard, and because of his good work record, he was again promoted. He became manager of the entire plant. And it was his undoing.

Within five years he suffered personal losses, including his health and his ability to relax and enjoy his family and recreation. Nothing much pleased him anymore. He became driven and withdrawn. The owner of the plant liked Randy because of his good work record and didn't realize the extent of his unhappiness.

Randy felt pushed and unappreciated. The pressure to perform at a level he hated had now taken its toll emotionally, mentally, and physically. He was a work fanatic out of necessity. He had to fight against the awful dread within his mind that he wasn't really adequate for the job. He often talked about the "old days." He would become nostalgic and talk about his youth and how he started out in life with very little, but he was quick to add how happy those days were.

If Randy had dared to listen to his own heart, he would not have become part of the management team. He would have stayed in the mailroom, where he was happiest. We feel a sense of accomplishment when we are promoted because we are taught when we are children to always strive for something better in life. We are taught that a successful person is one who makes something more out of what he began with. We tend to admire the man or woman who attains a high position when they started out on the bottom rung of the ladder. Unfortunately, we are not taught that sometimes the bottom rung of the ladder is an okay place to be. Randy finally did realize his need to go back to his old job, where he was happier.

Karl was a handsome young man whom everyone thought had a great future. When he was in high school he decided he was going to be a doctor. His decision was largely due to the influence of his parents. He was raised in a home where there was very little money, and he told friends he could hardly remember a time when he wasn't hungry. From the time he was a small boy his parents fed him with stories about becoming a rich doctor so people would look up to him. In spite of the social and financial handicaps that stood in Karl's way, he became determined to fulfill the goal his parents had set for him. He worked very hard in high school to get good grades, but when he entered college it soon became evident that he did not have the ability to get the grades needed to go on to a medical career. To the enormous dismay of his parents, he had to leave college.

When Karl quit school it was as though he quit life. He withdrew from his friends and closed himself up in his room. He rarely ventured out. He spent his time watching TV and sleeping. Because he had lost a goal which he identified with so strongly, Karl considered himself less than a nothing. He did not seize upon the message he was giving to himself—"I want something more! I want to be me!"—and use it as a point of self-discovery. Perhaps Karl would have made a very happy deep-sea diver or a very happy high school science teacher, or a very happy construction worker. Karl did not give himself a chance to find out the niche his life was created for. He committed suicide six months after leaving school.

## Knowing and Appreciating Your Needs

Prior to his death, Karl was appalled and crushed to learn his needs for success couldn't be met. He couldn't see beyond his being dropped from college. Karl's life had been led by the fantasy of becoming a rich doctor, and without his dream he believed he couldn't go on. Karl shows us how strongly our needs affect our behavior.

Experiments with animals placed in an obstruction box demonstrate the strong effect our needs have. Doctors George Lehner and Ella Kube, in their book *The Dynamics of Personal Adjustment*, give an example of an experiment made with an obstruction box with a mouse at one end and a piece of cheese at the other. Between the mouse and the cheese there is an electrically charged grid. If the mouse is fed just prior to placing him in the box, he will show only a perfunctory interest in the cheese. If the mouse is not fed and he is ravenously hungry, he will bend all his efforts to get the cheese, even risking contact with the charged grid, until he succeeds or falls victim to exhaustion.

Needs influence our behavior. It is important, then, to identify what we consider needs. The psychologically hurting person usually has unrealistic and destructive needs. You may think that you need to make a lot of money in order to be happy. If you believe this is a need then you will choose your work accordingly. It may be you will discover that your devotion to satisfying the need to make money will leave other needs in your life unsatisfied.

In his book *Mental and Elemental Nutrients,* Karl Pfeiffer tells of a study made by Dr. A. Hatch, in which isolated rats placed in an empty environment became caricatures of the lonely housewife. They gained weight, were jumpy and nervous, and showed signs of nervous disorder. The woman who believes her needs are centered on being taken care of by somebody else may find certain other needs in her life unmet.

When we become dissatisfied, bored, or frustrated, we lose interest in our own well-being. The very thing we thought was so crucial is now not even important. In the drive to be better than anyone else, we sacrifice very important personal needs.

## List Your Needs

A Staying Happy principle is to know your needs. Some needs you have are very basic, and it is important that they be met. Below is a list which you can examine regularly to make sure you are heading in the right direction. *Needs are not demands.* Too many patients in mental hospitals and too many patients in the offices of psychologists and psychiatrists are there because of a conflict of needs.

There is a difference between *need* and *want.* Locate what you are telling yourself you can't live without. Karl told himself he could not live without the dream of being a doctor one day. The truth is, he didn't think he could exist as a failure at meeting his own expectations and the expectations of others. Karl did not give himself a chance to discover what he would have liked to do with his life. He really didn't get to know or be himself. Socrates said, ''The shortest and surest way to live with honor in the world is to be in reality what we appear to be.''

In order to be in reality what you appear to be, you must know and be in control of your needs; otherwise your needs will control you. On one side of the page I am listing some realistic needs. These you should have fulfilled, and it is realistic for you to pursue them. On the other side of the page is a list of unrealistic demands. These demands are not needs but neurotic wants. You don't *need* them! Identify these statements in both columns.

| Realistic Needs | | Unrealistic Demands |
| --- | --- | --- |
| | | (Which means: I *must* have.) |
| Self-confidence | not | Power and authority |
| Friendship | not | Unquestioning loyalty |
| Respect | not | Adoration |
| Trust | not | Power |
| Love | not | Dependency |
| Skill | not | Brilliance-genius, *the best* |
| Thinking and reasoning ability | not | Dazzling mental abilities |
| Creativity | not | Masterful achievements |
| Freedom | not | Pampered pleasure |
| Self-discipline | not | License to sin |

How many of the above list of unrealistic demands do you recognize in your own life? Your Realistic Needs list is important. Write down your needs in your journal so that you can be aware of them and not deny yourself the privilege of having them met consistently in your life. If these needs are not met, you will feel frustrated. You won't know how to make the hurt of frustration go away. You will not only be frustrated but you will also feel you are among the disadvantaged and unlucky of the world. "Other people get all the breaks," you may grumble, just because someone else is a genius and you're not. Or you may complain how nobody loves you when actually you're saying someone isn't *adoring* you the way you demand to be adored.

## Recognizing Frustration and Dealing With It

Often your needs won't be fulfilled the moment they arise. If you have a need for respect and your teenager talks back to you, calls you a name, and goes sulking to his room, you may feel frustrated. I spoke earlier of the misguided need to make a lot of money and thereby postpone the fulfillment of other needs. The time lapse between need and the satisfaction of the need can be frustrating. Some needs can only be satisfied in the future. If you are a college freshman and you want to go on to law school, your goal is long-range, so you will want to have the other, more urgent needs fulfilled now, one of them being the need for self-confidence. If you feel you are not succeeding in reaching your goal, you will feel frustrated, so you will want to be sure you reward yourself often by having many of the above needs met. Frustration is no fun, and we usually feel frustrated when we think we are somehow being deprived or when our happiness is threatened. Psychologist Abraham Maslow stated in an article in the *Psychological Review* that it is important that we know the difference between deprivation and threat in order to understand our reaction to frustration.

What are you telling yourself? Maslow used the example of two children who are told they can't have an ice-cream cone. One child regards this as a case of being denied something good. He cries over it for a long time. The second child interprets the refusal as a sign the mother no longer loves him. One response is frustration because of being deprived and the other response is being frustrated and threatened with the personal loss of love.

## The Need for Discipline

Your need for self-discipline must be met if you are going to be a happy person. A frustrating situation can appear to be different at various times, depending upon whether you feel it is caused by some external force over which you have little or no control, or whether you feel you have made it happen by your own actions. According to Doctors Lehner and Kube, a student who comes to class late feels more at ease about his tardiness if he can attribute it to flooded roads rather than oversleeping. If you can blame your frustration on something other than yourself you won't feel guilty. Lack of discipline leads to frustration and self-loathing. I've never met a person without discipline who was truly delighted with life. Maybe you hate taking responsibility for your own happiness because you don't want to identify your needs. Discipline is a fruit of the Holy Spirit. It teaches you in a happy, protecting way to be responsible for your needs being met so you don't become frustrated.

**When in doubt about responsibility, take it.**

We will work overtime to disprove we have any needs at all other than a craving to feel important at the job. Another kind of person works desperately at not doing anything wrong and taking the blame for others. If someone else breaks a vase he apologizes for his clumsiness. If a friend loses a job, he will somehow feel responsible for not helping him keep it. If he loses his keys, he does penance by despising himself for such a stupid mistake and he will find ways to pay for his error without knowing he's doing it. He may call an expensive locksmith to open the door of his car or house, thereby being unable to go to the special concert or some other special event he had saved his money for.

To feel the least disruption, you must feel secure within yourself that your world will not fall apart when the fulfillment of your needs is threatened. If a demand is made or it looks as though you are going to be denied something, you may feel extremely upset and frustrated. You may then rationalize your problem or withdraw and deny it. (We will discuss both of these responses in detail in a later chapter.) Why work so hard to gain God's approval?

You belong to God and you are joined to Him forever. When you realize your first and primary need is to be one with Him, the other needs are answered. To look for self-worth without God is as hopeless as hunting for buttercups among the thorns. Jesus is Lord of your needs. Will you accept that reality right now before going any further? Free yourself now. Mother Teresa said in a *Time* magazine interview, "We must *free ourselves* to be filled by God."

Christian singer Dallas Holm explains it this way: "To not accept Jesus as your Lord is sheer craziness." Trying to fulfill needs in our lives without the Great Fulfiller really does make us crazy. Dallas Holm tells young people, "I'm not intimidated by the intellect of our age that would lead me away from God. There's nothing in this world worth missing Jesus over."

There is no need big enough to intimidate God or render Him helpless.

## Unrealistically High Goals

If your ideals and standards are unrealistically demanding, you may be prey to the enemies of "musts" and "shoulds" and "oughts." It's important to have goals and to have ideals, but when demands are excessive, they become hurtful and frustrating. We hurt when we feel our lives are not being lived as well as they could be. With your efforts and the help of the Holy Spirit, you can't fail.

A boy named Henry worked sixteen hours a day at his job as a gardener. Eventually he lost interest and the commitment he had to his work became shaky. His ideal was to do his work perfectly and better than anyone else, but he was uninterested now. Henry was not an underachiever. His goals were too high. His symptoms all pointed to a need to pull back, reevaluate, and start afresh.

An underachiever doesn't usually have problems with becoming a work fanatic. Achievement is one measure of fulfillment, and to the work fanatic it becomes a major measure of fulfillment. He or she feels achievement gives him or her the right to feel fulfilled. The person then sets goals which are overdemanding and require driving dedication—something a happy person knows better than to do.

## Expectations That Hurt

Bonnie is a woman who believed once she got out of the house and got a job her life would be filled with personal fulfillment and excitement. Her goals were high and unrealistic. She got a job working in an office in Greenwich Village, more than an hour from home. She was so delighted to land a job that commuting didn't bother her. She felt as though she had been let out of a cage when she was buying clothes to wear to her new job and preparing herself to be her own person at last. She had been known as wife and mother for so long she hardly knew how to accept her new role as Bonnie, the woman who commuted to work and produced effectively eight hours a day.

Bonnie expected her job to provide her with self-esteem and confidence the way her husband's work did for him. Her expectations were all-encompassing; she expected her job to provide her with fulfillment not only in her occupational life but in her personal life as well.

Bonnie had glamorized going back to work and believed she was entering a world far more exciting than the one she had been living in for so many years. She believed staying at home and raising children was a boring and thankless life. She believed that the women in the work force were the women who got all the rewards. In time, when she realized how unrealistic her expectations were, she was able to change. It wasn't easy for her to admit that working wasn't as much fun as she longed for it to be. It was tiring, low paying, and the people she worked with were unfriendly.

Anna had a different set of unrealistic goals. She saw herself as superwife and supermom. She concentrated all of her energies on her home and family, to the point where she actually went over the floor on her hands and knees looking for pieces of lint or dust when crossing a room. She baked, grew her own garden, sewed, and did everything she believed a true Proverbs 31 woman should do. If you were to hear her talk, you would hear sentences like, "I really *should* get over to the supermarket because there is a sale on artichokes," or "I *must* pick up those recipes from Margaret so I can start my canning early." Often she said, "I really *ought* to do that a little better. . . ."

Anna bought all of the women's magazines, watched cooking shows on TV, and ran her house the way a sergeant would run his platoon. The children were instructed in neatness, the godliness of cleanliness, the advantage of achieving, and the virtues of a job well done.

A minister tells me how he once craved to be needed. "When I first became involved in the area of pastoral care, I could concentrate on very little else. I was in love with the idea of being able to help someone." He programmed his own failure by failing to understand the definite limits in his skills and time. We each have to remind ourselves that we may not be able to handle every complex problem of every person who comes our way. There are many problems we can solve as Christians, and with God's help we can certainly accomplish far more than we could dream possible in our own strength. We cannot play God. At the root of unrealistically high goals is the sin of pride, when we believe we are God rather than allowing God to be God. In this way we all program ourselves for defeat.

## You Cannot Be All Things

The housewife, the minister, the woman back in the work force, the executive, or the doctor—none of them can be all things to all people. We cannot be all things to ourselves, either. Often the work fanatic with high expectations will think of himself as a person chosen and set apart to accomplish something so special and unique that God could only choose *him* to do it. This person is under pressure to achieve and succeed constantly. It is difficult for the work fanatic to relax without feeling guilty that he is wasting time.

Answer the following questions.

1. Do you feel guilty when you take time off from your work? _____

2. Do you feel you have overextended yourself more than not? _____

3. Do you consider yourself a competitive person? _____

4. When you do a good job, do you want recognition for it? _____

5. Do you feel impatient with delays or interruptions? _____

*If you answered yes to any of the questions above,* you may be trying to be all things. It's time to take a good look at yourself, your goals, and your motives for your work and personal life. If you answered yes to the first question, it may be that you will tend to overdo in order to do penance. The trap here is that if you feel guilty, you must be punished. Do you find it difficult to relax without feeling guilty? Are you more tense while vacationing or planning your social activities than at other times?

*If you answered yes to number 2* and you find yourself often overextended, your strong need for achievement may be in the category of the demand for recognition. Your health and happiness may be jeopardized because you feel it is necessary to *earn* the adoration and admiration of those around you.

*If you answered yes to number 3,* it may be that you have gone beyond the normal limits of competition. Everything is *not* a challenge. To think so is like mimicking a high school graduation address instead of living life with its disappointments and mediocrity as well as its joys and achievements.

*If you answered yes to number 4* and find that your desire for recognition is inordinate, look at the misbelief connected here. What you do and have may be your proof of your personal value. Jesus did not die on the cross for you so that you would have to earn your personal value throughout your life. You are a winner because you simply *are*.

*If you answered yes to number 5* and find yourself impatient with delays and interruptions, recognize the misbelief here, which is, "I must control everything around me and everything around me must be controlled by me." You cannot control the world. The world is full of delays and interruptions. You are not responsible for anyone's life but your own. If your own life is in control, your loved ones will benefit, as well as your colleagues and friends. Stress-prone people have very little patience with those who do not perform up to par. The work fanatic hates to be interrupted when he's charging full steam ahead.

Do you find it difficult to enjoy doing nothing? Louis L'Amour, the prolific and famous author of western novels, confessed, "The things I would do for fun are the things necessary to my work anyway. My work is also my hobby."

Does this sound like the utterance of a work fanatic? Actually Louis L'Amour is letting us in on a secret of his own self-discovery. He continues his confession with these words: "I am happiest when working."

## The Positive Power of the Work Fanatic

Not all work fanatics are miserable creatures of stress and overwork. The godly work fanatic is a doer who organizes his time, allows himself leisure, spends time alone, and loves his or her work. Greek philosopher Marcus Aurelius said, "Our life is what our thoughts make it." The work fanatic tells him or herself that it's fun to work. The work fanatic aims for a goal and achieves it. But as Logan Pearsall Smith wisely advised, "There are two things to aim at in life: first, to get what you want; and after that, to enjoy it. Only the wisest of mankind achieves the second.''

If you answered yes to more than two of the previous five questions, it's time to make some changes.

## STAYING HAPPY IN AN UNHAPPY WORLD EXERCISE FOR THE WORK FANATIC

Tell yourself these sentences:
- The real me does not depend upon achievement to feel good about myself.
- The real me is able to relax and enjoy my leisure time.
- The real me is a happy and contented person.
- The real me is a worthwhile person regardless of other people or relationships, jobs, work, ministry, health, or environment.
- I am a new person in Christ. All the old things have passed away.

Memorize this Scripture:

*Therefore if any person is (ingrafted) in Christ, the Messiah, he is (a new creature altogether) a new creation; the old (previous moral and spiritual condition) has passed away. Behold, the fresh and new has come!*
*2 Corinthians 5:17* AMPLIFIED

# FIVE

# The Perfectionist Seldom Finds Happiness

Cal is not happy. He thinks the unhappy world is to blame. He wonders how long he can go on with the way things are. He owns two used-car lots and also serves on the board of his church and teaches Sunday school. He works ten to twelve hours a day at his car lots, then often goes directly to the church to work until late at night. He feels he is doing mankind a great service but his wife suffers from loneliness and his children are becoming rebellious. Cal is angry when his wife and children place demands on him because he cannot understand why they are not more supportive of his dedicated fervor to provide well for them and to serve God. Cal sees himself as a giving, unselfish, faithful Christian, but actually Cal has a powerful narcissistic need to compensate for his inferiority feelings, which keep him from seeing the truth. Cal really does not like himself because as hard as he tries, he simply can't ever seem to be perfect.

As we saw in chapter 4, success can be very costly. The pursuit of success can be confused with a desire for happiness. Cal thought success and happiness meant being perfect. His problems intensified when he realized a very imperfect world would always get in his way.

Perfectionism is sometimes a nice way of saying "obsessive compulsive." *The Diagnostic and Statistical Manual of Mental Disorders* (DSM-III) describes the obsessive-compulsive personality as being "excessively rigid, overinhibited, overconscientious, overdutiful, and unable to relax easily."

A certain degree of obsessiveness is helpful to have when you need to be hardworking and conscientious. If you must meet a goal or deadline, a healthy amount of obsessiveness is beneficial. The industrious, organized, and efficient person knows it's important to be dedicated to doing a good job. It becomes out of balance if the person behaves overconscientiously and overdutifully, because then burnout is imminent.

## Obsessive Compulsiveness Isn't Always Bad

The times in your life when it is not neurotic to be obsessive-compulsive is when you are a student. Medical students, seminary students, and other graduate students would hardly get through the demands of school without being committed to their work to a degree that is over and beyond the call of normal everyday living. When you are hard pressed to accomplish a task, when you have a deadline at hand, when you are working on a project requiring more work than an ordinary job, and you find that you must work many more hours a day than usual, you are not necessarily behaving neurotically. Nor should you accept labels such as ''workaholic.'' There are some times in life when you must work harder than others. A problem develops if you're driven to perfectionism and find no satisfaction in your achievements because they only remind you of what's left to achieve.

When you are dedicated to being perfect, it is as though you can never be content with what you do. You are constantly critical of yourself and always striving to do better. Perhaps you learned this behavior as a child because the love you received from your parents was conditional. This is how it was for Dave, a young man studying for the ministry in the Bible school where I taught. Dave worked harder than anybody and his speeches and stories were always outstanding. He was critical of himself and after his speeches would ask his friends if they thought he was any good, if they had any suggestions, if they caught every point. He doubted that his speech could possibly have any merit if it was not the most perfect speech of the class. In examining some of Dave's background I learned that when he was a child he was always expected to live up to a certain standard. His parents had high expectations of him and if he brought home a report card with all *As* and one *B*, they would notice the *B* first. "Son, this is a good report card but why did you get only a *B* in calculus?

The perfectionist hates to think of himself as "average." The very idea of being an average person in an average world is boring and offensive. The thought of being ordinary makes the perfectionist nervous.

Perfection is an illusion which does not exist in our world. Only God is perfect. The harder you strive for perfection, the worse your disappointment will be because the concept of perfection is not compatible with reality. If you look at everything around you, notice that most of it can probably be improved upon. The room you're in now could probably be decorated better, the car outside might be able to use a paint job or at least a wash and wax, the trees in the park could possibly need pruning, the building next door may very well need renovation, your shoes may need shining, your nails need polishing, or your hair needs cutting.

I recently had lunch with a doctor friend of mine who told me he could never remember a time in his life when he felt he had been a truly good boy in his parents' eyes, or that he had accomplished all they had expected of him. Even when he became a doctor his mother said to him, "Well, I hope you'll become a specialist." My friend struggled for years with perfectionist attitudes.

Another kind of perfectionist is the one who takes no chances in life out of fear of making a mistake. This person will never function in extremes or excesses and will choose the middle of the road, where there is the least amount of conflict. My friend Shirley fits this description. She and I are opposites. When she takes a vacation, she wants to have every step and moment planned. She gathers all the material she can that's been written about the place she's going, and she must be absolutely sure she will not have to spend more money than she wants to. As for me, I would just as soon hop in the car and drive anywhere at all just for the sheer joy of doing something new and getting away to relax.

My friend is a "perfect person" type because she works hard not to offend anyone or call attention to herself, and she always does what is expected of her. She is dedicated to doing the "right" thing.

Shirley is completely predictable. I know she will not take any radical risks with her business or anybody else's. She will never do what is known on Wall Street as the "Venezuelan Trade." This is where a stockbroker takes a risk so dangerous that before making the deal, he buys a ticket to Venezuela. If the deal succeeds, he's rich. If he fails, he buys cab fare to the airport. Shirley always takes the path of least resistance, never a risk.

If you are a perfectionist like Shirley, you are guaranteed to be in constant turmoil. Do you continually strive to be perfect? Are you totally dedicated to the pursuit of perfection? Here is a quiz to test yourself with. It was developed by Dr. Hubert Hoffman, Director, Hillside Psychological Guidance Center, Queen's Village, New York. Answer the following questions with (A) Rarely, (B) Sometimes, or (C) Often. Then refer to the scoring and analysis that follow.

1. When writing a letter to a friend, do you rewrite it more than once to get it right? (A) _____ (B) _____ (C) _____

2. When dining out, do you find it necessary to wipe the silverware clean? (A) _____ (B) _____ (C) _____

3. When you've stayed out later than usual and come home dead tired, do you hang up your clothes before going to bed? (A) _____ (B) _____ (C) _____

4. When you're given a new recipe or get assembly instructions, do you follow the directions to the letter? (A) _____ (B) _____ (C) _____

5. When you stop at a service station for gas, do you have the air pressure in your tires checked? (A) _____ (B) _____ (C) _____

6. How frequently do you check with the telephone service to set your watch? (A) _____ (B) _____ (C) _____

7. When leaving home, do you double-check to make sure the doors are locked? (A) _____ (B) _____ (C) _____

8. If your child were having problems in school, would you assume you were somehow at fault? (A) _____ (B) _____ (C) _____

9. When you've had a bad dream, do you worry that it is prophetic of gloomy things to come? (A) _____ (B) _____ (C) _____

*Scoring.* Give yourself one point for each A answer that you gave; two points for each B answer; and three points for each C answer.

*9–14 points:* You could hardly be accused of being a perfectionist. In fact you have an enviable, laid-back approach to life which allows you to adopt a superrelaxed attitude toward your own—and other people's—shortcomings.

*15–21 points:* Normal range. You like to do your best, but don't punish yourself when you don't do as well as expected.

*22–27 points:* You are a full-blown perfectionist. This may cause some personal problems as you pursue unreasonable goals. You must first learn to accept yourself as a fallible human being. Instead of stewing over errors or failures, use them as learning experiences. When others fall short of your expectations, temper your criticisms with appreciation.

## Being a Selfish Perfectionist

If you are a perfectionist, you can be a very selfish person burying your emotions and working doggedly as an unconscious compensation for insecurities. Your perfectionism may be a means to fulfill your strong needs for approval. If you are a perfectionist, you are critical of yourself because you probably feel that you are an inferior person. You may spend most of your life working at a frantic pace to make a lot of money or to attain power or prestige in order to prove yourself, but what you are actually doing is trying to prove yourself to *yourself.* You want to prove to yourself that you aren't the loser you suspect you are underneath it all.

I like what Dr. David Burns does to combat the notion that we must be perfect. When he began jogging several years ago, he couldn't run more than two or three hundred yards in the hilly region where he lived. Most runners are taught to increase their distance and speed every day. Dr. Burns decided to make it his aim to run a little *less* than the day before. The effect of this was that he could always accomplish his goal easily. He would feel so good it would spur him on farther—"and every step was gravy," he said, "more than I had aimed for." Over a period of months, by daily practice he built up to the point where he could run seven miles over steep terrain at a fairly rapid pace. In this time he did not abandon his basic principle, which was to try to accomplish *less* than the day before.

If you will make goals for yourself that are not lofty to attain, you will not feel frustrated or disappointed. Instead of aiming for 100 percent, try for 80 percent, 60 percent, or 40 percent. The idea is to make a challenge of daring to be average.

What are the rewards for your dedication to perfection? Do you sense a life filled with enrichment? Perhaps you don't feel you are successful. One of my goals as we work through this book is to show you that no matter what level of life you are at, no matter what point you are now at in your career or family life, *your success depends upon what you tell yourself.* I would like to suggest that you make a decision to give up your perfectionism, at least on a trial basis.

If you want to be free of the viselike hold of perfectionism, look at your goals. Are they realistic? Is there anything that you have ever seen that is so perfect it could not be improved upon? What rewards have perfectionism brought you so far?

### Rewards I Think I Get for Being Perfect

1. I'll be perfect so I am the best I can possibly be at what I do, proving the Scripture, "Whatsoever you do, do with all your might" (*see* Ecclesiastes 9:10).

2. I'll make my parents proud.

3. I will feel satisfaction in a job well done.

4. Being perfect is what God expects of us.

### Proof That Being Perfect Isn't All That Rewarding

1. My drive to be perfect makes me competitive, critical, and unloving. I constantly judge other people's performance against what I believe is perfect. I am never happy, even when I do a good job.

2. I never *feel* my parents are truly proud anyhow, so why am I constantly trying to win their approval? It is God's approval I need, not any person's.

3. Exhaustion (not satisfaction) is more like it. Besides, I never feel I did the job well enough, no matter how exhausted I am.

4. Since I can't be perfect, I am constantly depressed. Is this what God wants for me?

5. People will give me more respect when I achieve things
   they admire.

Only God is perfect and His
Spirit within me makes me
like Him. I can trust myself to
reflect Him in my life.

5. I am so afraid of making mistakes that I really don't trust
   the respect people give me. I
   crave admiration but when I
   get it I don't really believe it's
   sincere because I'm not perfect.

## Your Motives

As the above chart shows, fear always lurks behind the drive to
succeed and to be perfect. Fear will cause you to become a raving
obsessive-compulsive person. Now let's look at motives. As you drop
your drive to be perfect, you will have to confront the fear that moti-
vates you. Criticism, failure, and disapproval can be so frightening
to you that you get quite upset at the thought of facing those
things. If you insist that everything you do is "just right" you may be
motivated by the fear of being criticized because you might make
a mistake.

## Curing Your Fear

When you discover motives characterized by fear, admit them and
face them. Here are two exercises to begin immediately:

1. Refuse to give in to your fear habit. No matter how upset or
   terrified you become, allow yourself to feel the emotional pain.
   It will disappear eventually.
2. You may feel as if you can't stand the unhappiness you're
   experiencing, but it is important to stubbornly refuse to give in.
   If you are afraid you left the door unlocked, you must *not* turn
   around to check it, if this has been a compulsive habit of
   yours. Perhaps you cannot stand to be alone in your house
   without being absolutely sure every door and window is
   locked. You're behaving irrationally if you check more than
   once.

Suppose you feel that you absolutely must make sure your house is spotless before your friends come over. When you have someone to dinner, you usually make sure every corner is clean and you fret over how good the dinner will be, what the table will look like, how the kids are dressed, and if everything is perfect and in place. As an exercise, go to your phone and invite somebody to dinner. After you have invited him or her over, be sure you do not give in to the urge for perfection. Prepare a simple meal. Resist the urge to frantically clean. Don't change clothes.

The fear of doing something wrong or of being found fault with is what you are combating by being easier on yourself. I know a couple who stopped inviting guests to their home because it was too nerve-racking. Each time they invited friends in they argued and were so tense in making preparations that when their guests finally arrived, they were exhausted. They told me it was simply easier for them not to have anyone over. The truth is, their demands on themselves to be perfect were simply too much.

A rigid approach to living can rob you of joy. A boy named Tim, sixteen years old and a sophomore in high school, would become a jangle of nerves when he was required to write a paper at school. Every time he had the assignment to write a paper, he went to bed with some unexplainable illness. His mother finally realized that he was not really physically sick, but something was wrong emotionally.

After talking with Tim, I understood why he was fearful of writing papers—indeed, fearful of school in general. His academic classes were the worst. The other classes did not cause him intense anxiety because the demands placed on him were minimal. He was able to get through by winging it, copying other people's work, and dropping courses. In time, even his easy courses began to show signs of his losing control. Physical Education, his favorite class, was now threatening. The Physical Education coach called his mother and told her Tim had been cutting class. The same went for his speech class. By the end of the semester Tim had flunked French, English, World History, and Physical Education. His mother was frantic. "I don't understand it. Tim has always been such a smart kid."

Tim's problem was not that he was lazy or uncaring. It was that he cared *too much*. He was gripped with such anxiety at the idea he might do a bad job that he did no job at all. Tim suffered with severe panic that something awful would happen to him if his work was bad. It started with his writing term papers because he was afraid of writing a bad paper. Often writers suffer from something called writer's block. This is a form of anxiety stemming from the misbelief "What if what I write is bad?"

In order for me to help Tim, he had to see that his problem was not that he had a learning disability but that he was afraid of failure. When I asked him to tell me who he especially admired in his life, he named superheroes whom he had never met. Tim also believed that his parents were perfect. He did not want to compete with his father, who was a successful lawyer, because he knew he could never outdo him. His father was a brilliant man who had graduated summa cum laude from Yale. Tim had been programmed to believe he, too, would go to Yale. Tim was terrified at the thought because he knew he was neither the hero nor the scholar his father was. Nearly everything Tim attempted to do was accompanied by the fear he wouldn't do it right. This fear made Tim behave disagreeably, irrationally, angrily, and he sought refuge in nonacademic activities.

Tim's friends were mostly ne'er-do-wells who had no ambitions in life. Many of them were deeply troubled young people who spent much of their day high on drugs. Because of Tim's low self-image, these were the people he identified with.

When Tim saw the fear which motivated him and began to realize that he was not the idiot he believed he was, we had made a giant step toward his well-being. Here are the negative thoughts Tim identified, as well as the words he told himself to counteract them.

1. If I fail, I'll be punished.

2. Everyone will know I'm really stupid.

1. Punishment does not always accompany failure unless I think in failure terms and unless I accept punishment. Even if I were punished in some way, I could probably handle it.

2. Everyone does something stupid once in a while. This

doesn't mean we're all worthless. I don't behave stupidly 100 percent of the time. I have the right to win the respect of my teachers and peers without being forced to win the best grades or do the best job.

3. My parents will hate me when they see how stupid I am.

3. My parents have nothing to do with it. It's me I'm the most concerned about. *I* will hate myself. Even if my parents did hate me, reject me, throw me out on my ear, I could go on to lead a productive life.

4. I really have nothing at all to say when I write a paper.

4. It isn't that I don't have anything to say; it's that I have not done my research and gathered information on a subject.

5. I must be perfect because it's the only way to be.

5. If I am not perfect and someone finds fault with me, it's his problem. I cannot be pleasing people all the time because it's too tiring. I do not have to be perfect because a belief in perfection makes my life tense, constricted, and miserable. I'm deciding now to set my own standards according to the Word of God and risk failure.

6. I'd rather do nothing than do something poorly.

6. This is do-or-die thinking. I can enjoy all that I do without comparing myself to what other people's standards of excellence are. Doing nothing at all is very frustrating to me and I'm sick of being afraid of disapproval. The worst thing that could happen to me, if I tried to change

my life, is that I might disap-
prove of myself. I choose to
concentrate on efforts rather
than the results. When I tell
myself I'd rather do nothing
than fail, I am only seeing the
results and I am forgetting
the efforts involved and the
joy of pursuit.

Negative thoughts containing no truth are often the reason we set
the wrong goals for ourselves. The secret to your success is to set
your goals less lofty so that you, like Tim, can experience the satisfaction of meeting goals. Clinging to perfectionism and the misbelief of
never wanting to make a mistake will help you procrastinate and do
absolutely nothing. Sometimes you may restrict social activities out of
fear of rejection. You may restrict your work activities out of fear of
making a mistake. It's important to know that it is impossible not to
make mistakes. Tim did change. It wasn't easy and it took a long
time, but he is now a senior in high school and he is getting *C*s and
*B*s. He feels good about himself.

## Change and Its Effects on Your Life

You can change your life when you choose to. If you want to add
zing and joy to your life, change may be the opportunity you need.
Each stage of your life poses change. You are always facing new
challenges, encouraged to develop new skills, meeting new problems
to solve. You can change when you see the need to change by locat-
ing the lies that you are telling yourself and by seeing how big a part
the Lord Jesus has in the stress you are experiencing. Most of the
time you will find the change you are craving is from acting and
believing carnally instead of acting and believing in the power of the
Holy Spirit.

Retrace your mental steps to the thoughts you fed to yourself
about an event you perceived as threatening. If you do not like your
response, change your mind immediately and choose a new point of
view: *I am precious.*

You can live successfully without clinging to the adolescent infatu-
ation with success. You can be aware of who you are, have great

dreams, and yet live a life of commitment and responsibility. Change means to look at the way you view your life and the world around you. The strengths and stresses of your life are the result of what you have programmed into your belief system. Your views about yourself, about God, your world, and what makes life worth living are the forces behind who you are and what you do. Change means examining the way you view the events of your life. You can change the amount of stress you suffer in seeking success by changing your perception of your life and of what makes success.

## STAYING HAPPY IN AN UNHAPPY WORLD EXERCISE FOR THE PERFECTIONIST

What, in your opinion, is success? _____

_____

Name two things you consider yourself a success at:_____

_____

_____

Name something you are going to do at the risk of failing: _____

_____

Finish the following: ''Dear Lord Jesus, thank You for delivering me from the self demands of perfectionism and for helping me to understand: _____

_____

_____

# SIX

# Staying Happy and Giving Up Denial

When I met Kathy for lunch on a sunny afternoon she was vibrant and talkative. She was eager to give me an account of how well her life was going, how happy the children were, and how productive her husband was on his job. She told me several times through the course of our lunch that the Lord was showing her many new things and that she was in a wonderful time of learning.

I didn't catch the clue she was giving me right away. I suspected something was amiss, but it became evident only when Kathy said, "Oh, by the way, I have to go into the hospital tomorrow for breast surgery. My doctor is worried about a lump he found and wants to remove it."

She told me this smiling and fidgeting with her fork. As a therapist, I have learned the things people tell me last are usually the things they consider most important. "Kathy, I want to be there with you. Would that be all right with you?"

Suddenly Kathy dropped her fork and her face lost its shine of carefree contentment. "Oh, will you, Marie? I'm not worried, of course, because I know God will be with me, but it will be very comforting to know you will be there, too."

Kathy did not want me to think she was the least bit nervous. She denied that there could be anything upsetting at all about the possibility of having breast cancer. Her denial of her anxiety and fear would actually cause her more fear and anxiety in the long run.

Psychologist Karen Horney, in her book *The Neurotic Personality of Our Time*, said there are four main ways of escaping anxiety:

1. To deny it.
2. To avoid the thought or feeling which arouses it.
3. To rationalize it.
4. To narcotize it.

Denial is a powerful defense against facing our fears and negative feelings. My friend Kathy did not want to face her fears of cancer, so she denied she was feeling anything at all except a blithe concern and faith that all would be well. Denial consists of an attempt to disavow the existence of unpleasant reality. Any perception of a painful nature can be denied. Some of the denials we engage in are the following:

## Denial of Fear

"Scaredy-cat, scaredy-cat," children may call each other. From our earliest recollections we hear words such as, "Don't be afraid. Be a brave little soldier." But we also learn that there are many things to be genuinely afraid of. On the one hand our parents tell us to be brave, but on the other hand they teach us to be frightened with statements such as, "Don't go in the street or you might get killed."

Recognizing and admitting fear is the first step to overcoming and neutralizing it. Sometimes we deny a fear we are not even aware of. This kind of fear holds enormous psychological power because we're trapped in a web of being unable to do something about a fear we don't even know. French philosopher Montaigne said, "My life has been full of terrible misfortunes—most of them which never happened."

Another denial of fear is found in the person who constantly puts his or her life in some kind of danger. "I'm not afraid of pain," might be the words of a person denying fear. A young teenager faces a menacing group of enemy teens all by himself. The boys approach him with hate written all over their faces, but the lone teenager stands his ground and says hotly, "You don't scare me." An American novelist said, "Life, as it is called, is for most of us one long postponement. And the simple reason for it is: FEAR."

To deny yourself the right to experience fear is denying yourself the right to *be*. All of your emotions are important. James Thurber tragically admitted, "Unfortunately, I have never been able to maintain a consistent attitude toward life or reality, or toward anything else. This may be entirely due to nervousness." Nervousness is a second cousin to fear.

*Fear of being alone.* When you deny a fear of being alone, you will fill up your life with countless trivial activities and meaningless relationships. Denying the fear of being alone can produce great conflict within you because you will call yourself an outgoing person and convince yourself you love people when actually you're simply afraid of yourself. Alone? You're *never* alone. You are *with* yourself.

The person who is afraid to be alone and denies that fear can become most self-engrossed. People will pity themselves and continue to pity themselves even when things are going well and their prayers are answered. Being alone is a good thing, actually. Imagine if Beethoven's Ninth Symphony had been written by a committee of composers. Can you imagine Shakespeare's *Midsummer Night's Dream* as a collective effort? Could Michelangelo's *Pieta* have been sculpted as magnificently if it had been done by a group?

It's time we faced our solitude with joy. Being alone does not mean being rejected or alienated. It means we are *with* ourselves. Dale Carnegie said, "For better or worse, you must play your own little instrument in the orchestra of life." You must remember that in God's orchestra we are all soloists.

The world around you is not like a cruel parent, with you the helpless, lonely child. When you are feeling depressed and empty inside, finding someone to fill up your hours with or to give you attention is not the solution. Realize the denial of the fear of being alone is the fruit of your human spirit.

The Holy Spirit within you tells you you are never alone because He is with you always. You can dare to fill your hours concentrating on the presence of God and telling yourself the truth. *Begin by admitting* you are afraid to be alone for a long time. There is no crime in being afraid to be alone. Once you have admitted your fear, you can begin to change.

*Fear of responsibility.* Terry is thirty-seven years old and has held more jobs than he can count. He has recently been fired from his latest job and is now looking for another. Each time he is fired, quits, or is laid off, he has a reason and it is always an excuse for his fear of responsibility.

Terry reminds me of the circus lion in the play *Don Quixote,* who longed to be free from his cage, out in the open air. One day the cage was accidentally left open and the lion leaped out to freedom. Once out, the weight of all that responsibility and freedom suddenly hit him and in confusion and fear, he turned and ran back into the cage.

Freedom requires responsibility to stay that way. Sometimes it seems easier to suffer and be in bondage than it is to make the effort to maintain freedom and happiness. The word *anhedonia* means "diminished ability to experience satisfaction and pleasure." For the person with a fear of responsibility who denies this fear, anhedonia can become a permanent way of life. The fear of responsibility for staying content and feeling good keeps you in a state of being unable to experience satisfaction and pleasure.

If you are afraid to be responsible, you will always find fault with yourself no matter how much you achieve or how much you do. If you refuse to admit this fear, you deny it. Denying fear does not make it go away.

It's important to give yourself the right to feel. Parents who tell their children, "Stop crying this minute!" or "Don't laugh so hard," or "Stop acting sad," are teaching them that feelings are bad. Possibly you respond to pleasure and happiness intellectually rather than emotionally, but you have the right to your good feelings and your bad feelings. God is a part of all of you, not just the you when you feel good. Those negative feelings, those fears and worries, are important and deserve your attention. Imagine yourself staying happy for several days in a row. Imagine yourself being responsible for your own happiness. You are in control and you can handle happiness.

## Denial of Anger

The nice person who loves being liked can often become bottled up with anxieties and frustration. Virginia is a person who fits this description. She and her husband came in to see me, and after talking with them both I was impressed with the enormous amount of denying of emotions both of them did. They were Christians, heavy drinkers, frustrated, and complained of several physical disturbances including gastrointestinal problems and headaches. Virginia told me she had never argued with her husband.

Their family was having a problem with a lack of communication. Their oldest son was failing in college, stealing money from his parents, using the family car carelessly, and behaving with hostility and rebellion at home.

Virginia's problem was her denial of anger. She simply could not admit that she felt the emotion of anger. As a child, it was so terrible for her to witness anger because of an overbearing and volatile mother that she snuffed any sign of anger within herself and stuffed it back into her psyche so that it never had to release itself in angry behavior. You don't hide anger, however. If you feel anger, you feel it. It doesn't matter whether you show it or not, you are feeling it. *Hiding anger does not make it go away.*

Virginia had spent a lifetime avoiding and hiding her anger, and she acted it out in many physiological, as well as psychological, expressions. Her fear of hurting people had reached phobic proportions by the time she came to me for therapy.

You have a right to your feelings. When you avoid facing your feelings, you are denying them. It is wonderful to experience the fruit of the Spirit of God, but by denying negativity, you rob yourself of the opportunity to work toward godly feelings. Negative feelings can be painful but they won't kill you, and you *can* change them.

If you open yourself up to disappointments and hurt, you can do it with skill and control. Being vulnerable does not mean you don't care. Virginia told me, "If I got angry, it would mean I didn't care about anything anymore. If I showed my husband I was angry with him because he wouldn't ever let me do anything without him, it would mean I didn't love him anymore and didn't care what he said to me."

This is denial: denial of responsibility, denial of anger, and denial of her own self-worth.

Expression of godly anger is very important. It can be done assertively by confronting and discussing your feelings with the person you feel angry at. Blowing up, letting off steam, and having temper tantrums aren't the best ways of handling anger. In fact, in one experiment headed by Dr. Jack Hokanson of Florida State University, it was found that expressing anger was helpful but *only* under certain conditions. Men angry at men was one situation studied, and the research showed that aggression was cathartic, and the blood pressure of furious *male* students would return to baseline more quickly when they could vent their hostility against the *man* who had angered them. This was only if the anger was expressed by and to a *man*. If the male student wanted to express anger to a teacher, it was far too anxiety-arousing to alleviate stress or be cathartic. Hokanson's research also showed that women do not treat anger the same as men treat it. When women anger women, it's a different situation. If a woman is insulted she doesn't ordinarily get belligerent; instead she will say something friendly to calm down the woman who angered her. For a woman any aggression is upsetting, much the same as a male is upset with aggressive behavior toward authority.

Anger expressed aggressively and furiously is a learned reaction, not an instinctive one, according to this study. If somebody irritates you and you lose control and swear or hit or pound something, there is a cathartic effect. This doesn't mean you'll be less angry in the future or that you are teaching yourself positive methods of handling anger. It means you are learning to do the same thing again. Temper tantrums are usually what the person is afraid of when he or she denies the emotion of anger.

Most theories now point to the fact that anger and its expression requires an awareness of choice. The first choice is to stop denying it. Everybody gets angry sometime. The old adage is, any emotional arousal will eventually diminish if you just wait long enough. Dr. Leonard Berkowitz of the University of Wisconsin has studied the social causes of aggression and claims yelling is no cure for anger. Dr. Berkowitz says, ''Frequently, when we tell someone off, we stimulate ourselves to continued aggression.''

It is not always the healthiest thing to scream and yell when you get angry. There are other solutions:

1. Be quiet and think calm thoughts before speaking or doing anything about your anger.

2. Discuss your feelings rather than screaming and yelling.
3. Admit your anger and tell yourself you are not a bad person for feeling angry.

Someone once said a person who cannot feel and express anger is a person who cannot feel and express love. Know that all of your feelings are important.

*Denial of a fear of worthlessness.* Being happy and staying happy in an unhappy world means to consider yourself in the light of your own achievements. Sandra is one of the most accomplished people I know. She worked her way through college and graduate school. She earned a master's degree in English and another one in Fine Arts. She teaches college English and creates art in her studio. Her paintings and sculptures are in collections and galleries all over the country. She is a creative woman with a stimulating personality. Sandra, however, constantly fights feelings of worthlessness. She often says things like, "I don't seem to be able to do anything right."

The truth is, Sandra does a lot of things right. So do you. If you tell yourself things such as, "Other people do things a lot better than I do," you need to stop and consider what you're saying. The truth is that a lot of times you do things very right. Sometimes you do things wrong. If you look at your life you could possibly tally up a lot more on the *right* side than the *wrong*. You spend a lot more time and effort and give a lot more attention to the wrong than to the right—like Sandra.

I went to a gallery opening where Sandra's work was being shown and I was overjoyed to see the response to her art. The critics raved and she sold a lot of work during the run of the show. Was Sandra happy? Here's what she told me the night of the opening: "Marie, this may be the end of my art career. I don't know how I could have been so stupid as to allow myself to agree to this show. When I see my work here now I see it's not anywhere near as good as I thought it was."

At times, when you hear people putting themselves down needlessly you want to give them a good punch and tell them, "Knock it off! How can you be so blind? Can't you see things are *wonderful* for you now?'' Comments like this would not have helped Sandra. Her terror at being discovered a worthless person precluded her ability to enjoy her success. She had lived a lifetime of denying her fear of worthlessness. In order to hide it, she achieved more. Her achievements really threatened her wishes for infantile caretaking and dependency. She felt people appreciated her work but *she* wasn't appreciated. How could she be appreciated when she felt she was so worthless?

Feelings of worthlessness must be admitted, felt, discussed, faced, and examined. Feelings of worthlessness must be counteracted with discussion and evidence that says the contrary. Sandra achieved much in her life. She goes on achieving even now. In order to avoid anxiety about her feelings of worthlessness, she felt she must achieve. Material gains and success were not important to her and they only increased her sense of hollowness and magnified her fears. She reminded me of this little rhyme I read once and never forgot:

> *Two men looked out from*
> *prison bars,*
> *One saw the mud,*
> *one saw the stars.*

Sandra kept herself stuck in the mud in every way. She found freedom from fear through hard and concentrated effort. That night at the gallery opening I suggested she find one thing, just one thing, no matter how small, to really be excited about and to enjoy.

"It's the end of my career," she moaned. Sandra's habit of overgeneralizing and "terriblizing" was part of her thought system.

## Overgeneralizing

Charles S. Carver and Ronald J. Ganellen of the University of Florida at Gainesville wrote an article for the *Journal of Abnormal Psychology* on why people get depressed. They devised a test to prove three attitudes that may lead to depression: trying to meet impossible standards, being too harsh on oneself in instances of failure, and overgeneralizing, when a person allows individual failures to make him feel worthless through and through.

Carver and Ganellen determined through their studies that over-generalizing was the strongest attitude on their depression index. Many of the people who were depressed could actually function on a daily basis.

You may be a person who often feels worthless. If you deny these feelings, you may tend to overachieve. Your achievements might be exactly the same as those of a person who has a lot of self-confidence. The difference is, you don't believe what you're doing is really worthwhile. Dr. Aaron Beck, director of the Center for Cognitive Therapy, conducted a test with depressed patients and nonde-pressed patients. The experiment was set up so that each group would succeed in half of the test and fail in the other half. Afterward the depressed patients discussed what they had *failed*. The nonde-pressed patients discussed their *successes*.

Denial of fears are a root of unhappiness. No matter how well you do something, how many achievements and accolades you stack up for yourself, if you have fears rumbling around unacknowledged or un-tended to, you will never fully enjoy the blessings that are yours.

One person is as happy as can be earning twelve thousand dollars a year. Another person earns thirty thousand a year and is utterly miserable with himself and his life.

What you feel yourself about *yourself* is what determines your happiness. You must begin to look at your life as a personal journey. When you avoid confrontation with yourself it does not matter how much beauty or goodness you've got around you—you won't be happy. Withdrawal into yourself can become a form of negation that simply helps you to avoid facing the truth.

The truth is that you are a wonderful person with lots of worthwhile abilities and attributes. When you refuse to face the reality that you are basically a valuable and precious human being, you are living a lie. Precious and valuable human beings make mistakes. The lie is that a person is not precious or valuable if he or she makes mistakes, does something stupid, doesn't look good, is too fat or too thin, fails at a lot of tasks, or procrastinates.

Denial is lying. It is avoiding, distorting and negating the truth. Psy-chologist Virginia Satir wrote a poem called ''I Am Me.'' She wrote it for a twelve-year-old girl who was deeply troubled. The girl asked her helplessly and desperately one day, "What is life all about anyway? Life makes no sense. What's the meaning of it all?" Dr. Satir's answer was her poem and one of the lines reads, "Because I own all of me, I can become intimately acquainted with me. By so doing, I can love me and be friendly with me and all my parts."

When you choose to believe Galatians 2:20, then your spirit becomes one with this fact. When you seek God only for His blessings, you sometimes can be disgruntled. When you seek Him for Himself and His miraculous power within you, you enter into that power.

### STAYING HAPPY IN AN UNHAPPY WORLD
### EXERCISE TO OVERCOME DENIAL

1. List some fears, such as the fear of someone finding out a secret of yours. Give this to Jesus, who said His burden is light (Matthew 11:30).

2. Give yourself the right to your feelings and write aome down, both negative and positive.

3. Ask Jesus to touch the negative feelings and create something new and beautiful out of them.

4. Write down two rationalizations you are going to change forever.

# SEVEN

# How to Overcome Guilt

# Forever

Suppose someone tells lies and false stories about you. What would your first response be? Hurt? Anger? Would you reason yourself out of hard feelings? Would you cry, get sick, try to figure out what you did to deserve such treatment? Would you dismally ask, "*Why* did he say such things about me? It's not fair." Would depression overtake you as you wonder why God permitted such injustice to be meted out to you?

There's more than the false rumors hurting you. If you would lose sleep worrying and pondering over and over again the injustice of the words spoken against you, there's another very painful condition at hand and it's not just your hurt ego. Ruminating the false stories over and over in your mind, talking to others about them, and in general, feeling emotional hurt and anger without relief brings you to the point of an insidious unspoken misbelief: *The false story is terrible and so am I.*

You think you are angry at the people who lied about you or accused you of something you didn't do—but look who you punish! Who suffers with your obsessive ruminating? The answer is *you* and only you. Misplaced anger hurts *you*. If you punish yourself for something you didn't do, you're a guilt slave. You may inwardly believe you deserve to hurt because only losers get lied about.

We are going to look at two kinds of guilt in this chapter: *misbelief guilt* and *godly guilt.* The above is an example of misbelief guilt. You act and feel just like a guilty person when in actuality you are not guilty. Misbelief guilt accompanies the lie that there is something wrong with you as a person.

When you experience misbelief guilt it is because you not only believe you make errors and mistakes (true) but you also believe that your errors and mistakes make *you* (false). We have already learned that our thoughts are our primary source of our unhappiness. Your unfounded feelings of guilt can show your misdirected anger. The bad names you were called are not true, but you see yourself as bad just because they were said. You may feel anger toward someone important to you but feel afraid to express it, so you turn it inward at yourself. It follows, then, that when bad things happen out of your control, you make sure you suffer and hurt to the maximum of your ability.

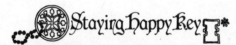

**Recognize feelings of anger and learn to confront them before turning anger inward toward yourself.**

Misbelief guilt tells you that only terrible people get angry or feel the negative feelings you do. You feel anger so you must be terrible, you think. But that may be too painful for you to face, too awful to confront; after all, nice people don't get angry at a loved one such as _____, do they? Nice *people don't have bad things said about them; oh, Lord, why me? Why am I so bad?* may be your unspoken dread.

Misbelief guilt masks important feelings you may have, such as anger, jealousy, bitterness, fear, and a host of others that cry for your attention. Because no emotion stands completely alone, guilt will also be accompanied by depression, shame, anxiety, and nervousness. Misbelief guilt doesn't reflect your behavior; it directs itself at you as a person. It doesn't only tell you that your behavior is bad—it tells you that *you* are bad as well.

If you do commit a sin or if you do something you are not pleased with, you'll feel guilt, and with it will be the lie that you are not a good person.

Misbelief guilt doesn't take much stock in forgiveness. In fact, if you're caught up in the trap of misbelief guilt, you may disregard forgiveness entirely.

### Forgiving Yourself

See your mistakes as something you *do*. The Bible tells us you and I are sinners and come short of the glory of God because we are human. In our human state we are going to make errors. If God is compassionate toward you, can you have mercy on yourself?

To be forgiven by God is to experience release from the grip of guilt. It is liberating beyond description to suddenly be free of the agonies and pain of a guilt-ridden mind. The past is no longer a present torment; you can be free of reliving your past sins as well as the sins of others.

Can you forgive yourself?

God does not want you to live under a burden of guilt. The Psalmist tells us, *"If thou, Lord, shouldest mark iniquities, O Lord, who shall stand? But there is forgiveness with thee . . ."* (Psalms 130:3, 4). The biggest culprit and worst offender in your life is not someone outside yourself—it is you. You are the one who tells yourself you are bad or unworthy. You are the one who believes what you tell yourself. Jesus said, "But if ye forgive not men their trespasses, neither will your Father forgive your trespasses" (Matthew 6:15). *The first person you must forgive is yourself.*

God forgives you and you can, too. Let's change our thought patterns, using the basic formula Dr. William Backus and I outlined in our book *Telling Yourself the Truth*. In it we show you how to examine your self-talk step-by-step and in detail. I want you to see how to discover the root of guilt:

1. *Identify* what you are telling yourself to produce guilt feelings. Is what you are telling yourself *true?* Can you ask God to forgive you?
2. *Challenge* the self-defeating lies you tell yourself with the truth and challenge yourself to accept forgiveness.

3. *Replace* the lies you tell yourself with constructive words of God's power and love.

Here are some sentences you may be telling yourself now or perhaps have in the past. I've challenged and replaced them with Staying Happy words of power and new life:

### I Feel Guilty Because

### Staying Happy Words of New Power

1. I have failed.

1. I will stop thinking the failures of my past are a permanent noose around my neck. God can turn my mistakes into miracles if I let Him. I have failed; I'm sorry I failed; but I'm forgiven and ready to be blessed!

2. I have acted dishonestly.

2. I can face myself, my weaknesses, my faults, and every problem I have. I am dishonest when I don't believe in my own self-worth. There is nothing wrong with being me. I am precious to God and all that I do has value. I ask God's forgiveness for not being grateful I'm me and for not expecting myself to be honest in all situations and circumstances.

3. I feel jealousy toward people so I gossip about them.

3. Guilt and self-condemnation are the result of my wanting to control others. I have wanted others to be less than I. I have needed to stand out and gain positive attention. I am not fully aware that there is nothing wrong with this desire so I feel the urge to control and dominate the success of others. Instead of allowing my drive for attention and my

feelings of jealousy to be expressed by gossip, I now choose to gain attention in godly ways, such as saying kind and loving things about others even though I may not think they deserve it. I forsake jealousy in the name of Jesus and choose to thank and praise God for His care and concern for us all.

4. People hurt me and I hurt them back.

4. I can be willing to be hurt a little, if necessary, in living a godly and giving life. I do not demand that all the world love and cherish me with unflagging devotion. If I give others the right to dislike me, and to at times be genuinely unloving to me, I will be free of needing the approval of others. The fear of being hurt no longer enslaves me.

5. I'm late a lot; I talk too much; I overeat; I'm irresponsible . . .

5. Negative behaviors indicate negative self-feelings. These behaviors are signals to myself. If I overeat, I may be telling myself I'm frustrated and upset. The Lord Jesus is my bread of life. If I am late, perhaps I'm afraid of the people or the place where I am going. Perhaps I'm behaving in a childish way instead of an adult way regarding my responsibilities. Jesus can deliver me from this. Perhaps I'm too busy and the message I am giving myself is to allow Jesus, by His Spirit, to clear out my work schedule. I can choose the power of

*God in my life. I no longer
allow myself to be deceived.
I no longer allow irrational
and fearful thoughts to make
me guilty. God is my rock
and my salvation, my stronghold: I shall not be shaken.*

Misbelief guilt makes you a guilt slave. The word *slave* is appropriate because guilt becomes your master. When guilt is in the background influencing your movements and thoughts, you're a slave. But
here's another kind of guilt that is crucial to recognize and act upon:
godly guilt. It's quite different from misbelief guilt.

*Godly guilt* tells us we have done something wrong and God wants
us to clear it up. The Christian is called to live a "holy and blameless"
life. Colossians 1:22 NAS tells us, "He has now reconciled you in His
fleshly body through death, in order to present you before Him holy
and blameless and beyond reproach." Feeling guilty about sin is
godly guilt and it must be recognized. If you are afraid to face your
sin, the feelings of guilt will increase and you may begin to act in ways
that are very harmful to you and to your own happiness.

Ginger was a thirty-five-year-old woman who had been behaving
with increasing irritability at home. She was angry, hostile, and bitter
toward her family and others around her. Her husband thought she
might be going through her change of life but in fact, that was not the
case. After I talked with Ginger at length, she told me, "Everything in
my life has just fallen apart. I feel as though there's nothing to look
forward to. Nothing means anything to me anymore."

I had to ask what had turned a vivacious and loving woman into
this gloomy and hopeless-talking person. I questioned Ginger and
discovered she harbored many misbeliefs such as the statement "I
think I've always been depressed." She hadn't always been depressed but her present unhappiness was so overwhelming to her
that she had lost a sense of a happy past or hopeful future.

I asked Ginger if she could tell me specifically when she began to
feel the depression she was experiencing now, but she couldn't tell
me. This was denial behavior because it was painful to be specific to

herself about her hurt. It was less painful to deny what was difficult to face up to. The pain of recognizing her behavior for what it was could be avoided by denial. "I suppose I started feeling bad a couple of years ago, if not before."

I wanted her to be specific. "Do you mean two years ago? About the time your husband started that new job?"

"Yeah, I guess that was about the time. He started working all those overtime hours. . . ."

I asked Ginger to tell me about herself at that time. She burst into tears and very reluctantly, after telling me about other people, her children, her own sense of alienation and identity problems, did she confess that she had met another man and had been attracted to him two years ago when her husband began working overtime. The guilt began and Ginger's world started to crumble. Her guilt mounted but the attraction to the man grew. "I couldn't stop myself!" she cried.

Her behavior then became so distorted that even her friends remarked about it. "Ginger used to be so sweet," people had said. "Now she is so edgy and critical. She's no fun anymore." When Ginger overheard these words she was crushed and her sense of alienation was, in part, punishment for her behavior, which she felt was unforgivable.

She dreamed of leaving her husband and running off with the "other man," but she knew she couldn't do that because the other man was not only unreliable but he was also a notorious Don Juan in the new neighborhood they had moved to.

Misbelief guilt is telling yourself how sinful and terrible *you* are, when you have every right to be happy and forgiven. Godly guilt tells you that you really are behaving badly or sinfully, and you need to take yourself to Jesus immediately to receive forgiveness and a new understanding and attitude.

God not only forgives your behavior but He also forgives *you*. He cleanses *you* from head to toe, inside out. Your biggest mistake in guilt is to confuse your behavior with your "self," and to believe that because you did a certain act, you *are* that kind of person. That is what Ginger believed. She believed that because she had sinned, she was through-and-through an immoral, untrustworthy, unregenerate, miserable excuse for a human being.

Ginger had to unearth the lies she had told herself and take a long and hard look at them. She had to face the Lord Jesus with her sin and ask forgiveness. She felt genuine godly guilt. She needed the words "Lord, cleanse me! I repent! I turn from sin and turn toward Your loving heart!" before she could begin the road to healing and staying happy.

Ginger tried paying for her own sins in a variety of hurtful ways: self-hate, depression, non-Christian friends, even sickness. It didn't work. Excessive godly guilt often attempts to atone for sins and wrongs of the past, but it can't and won't ever succeed. Ginger physically acted out her guilt and started a series of trips to the doctor for various ailments of the stomach and lower back. Her guilt had turned to self-hate. She felt trapped in the body of a despicable person.

Ginger's guilt about her feelings for a man other than her husband led her to behaviors that only compounded her guilt. Like the thief who says, "I'll go to jail anyway for past crimes, one more won't hurt," Ginger masked her intense hostility and helplessness with words like "Who cares? Why not? What difference does it make?" and the most deadly of all false statements, *"God doesn't care anyhow, so why not just do my own thing?"*

## The Past

For some of us, the past is unfinished. The past is still unburied and we continue to live in the shadow of yesterday. Disappointments and losses of childhood and youth haunt us as we neurotically try to redeem the past as well as demand we be compensated for our pain.

What do we feel guilty about? The frustrations and unmanageable events of the past may keep you from fully accepting the good you have right now in your life. You may still be punishing yourself for a past failure. Learning Staying Happy skills means you understand that even though you've been hurt, cheated, robbed, ignored, betrayed; stood helplessly by watching your dreams shatter and your most precious possessions lost, you can learn to live well and happily.

If your dreams have been unrealized and you've been hurt time and again, you can still accept today as yours. Your self-restricting, self-punishing behavior only keeps you bound to pain. You don't have to have your own way and you can stop your war against the world and yourself for not giving you your own way.

Your pain hurts and my pain hurts. Nobody has less or more to lose than someone else. You may feel bad but you can live with that. Can you live in a world that refuses to submit to you? Make room for the present. Face your losses and you'll face guilt square in the face.

If you commit a sin such as stealing, it is reasonable to accept the notion you could feel guilty about it later on, especially if you're caught. But what about failure? Do you realize you feel worse about failure and loss than about almost anything?

There is a wonderful saying we can learn from:

*There are two kinds of sorrow . . . when a man broods over the misfortunes that have come upon him, when he cowers in a corner and despairs of help—that is a bad kind of sorrow. . . . The other kind is the honest grief of a man whose house has burned down, who feels his need deep in his soul and begins to build anew.*

Living in the sorrows and failures of the past must come to an end. Your reactions to your past need to be identified. Ask yourself the question "What am I telling myself about my *past?*" Ask yourself, "What am I telling myself about my past hurts and failures?" Are you telling yourself any of the following?

- I didn't do what I should have done and that's terrible.
- I did what I thought was right but it failed and that's terrible.
- My dreams have been lost and a person without a dream is terrible.
- I have been rejected and so that means I'm terrible.

If you are telling yourself any of the above, write the following in your journal: Today I told myself the following lie: _____

_____

which is ridiculous, untrue, and unacceptable.

Guilt and hurt are closely related. We feel bad because we tell ourselves to feel bad. We think bad people feel bad; good people don't feel bad. If you *feel* bad it follows (illogically) that you *are* bad. "If I hurt I must be bad and I feel guilty about being so bad" is the unspoken nonsense.

You may have learned some other malarkey that is equally untrue, such as, "If you feel depressed it's because there's sin in your life," or "If you are really a good person you'll be a happy person," or "Sinners without Jesus are miserable and unhappy, but we Christians are joyful and happy at all times." These statements, if you believe them, will produce feelings of misbelief guilt and you'll be unhappy. Here are some common reasons you may give yourself to feel guilty without realizing the harm you are doing to yourself:

*Reasons I Choose to Be Guilty and*
*Some Staying Happy Responses*

| **How I Feel Guilty** | **Staying Happy Responses** |
|---|---|
| 1. I didn't do/I should have done: | Forgive me, Jesus. |
| 2. I did do and failed: | Forgive me, Jesus. |
| 3. I am bad because my situation fits both 1 and 2 | |

Complete the rest of the sentences that follow. Notice these forgiveness statements:

4. I ruined my relationship with: _____
Forgive me, Jesus.

5. I contributed to the unhappiness of: _____
Forgive me, Jesus.

6. I didn't do the wise thing when: _____
Forgive me, Jesus.

7. I don't do enough for: _____
Forgive me, Jesus.

8. I take more than I give to: _____
Forgive me, Jesus.

9. I shirk my responsibility regarding: _____
Forgive me, Jesus.

10. I'm in debt and that bothers me because: _____
Forgive me, Jesus.

## How Guilt Robs Your Happiness

Bill was a young man who grew up trying to meet the rigid expectations and standards imposed by his parents. He received extreme punishments for his mistakes and little appreciation for his achievements. He was rarely, if ever, praised or encouraged when he did well. Now Bill feels guilty about doing poorly before he even attempts to do a thing. He has taught himself to feel guilty and pessimistic toward life and himself. He blames himself for his bad feelings, which makes him angry. He then attempts to punish himself because he doesn't think it's Christian to feel angry. Bill believes that bad behavior should be judged and punished and since nobody knows what's going on in Bill's mind except Bill, he punishes himself by putting himself down and feeling guilty. He believes he can't do anything right, and that makes him feel unworthy of blessings and happiness. If you were Bill's counselor, what would you tell him? His problem is clearly not godly guilt, is it? Bill would find great relief as well as a new heart and mind if he were to realize he's a new creature in Christ despite what his parents taught him. His behavior is *his* responsibility now, not his parents'.

Nobody likes facing mistakes and admitting being at fault. We would rather blame others—anybody except ourselves. The first people we attribute our problems to are our parents. It may be true that they made some very big mistakes parenting us, but a key truth I always share is that the events of the past, as well as the feelings of the past, need not hold you back today. Your responses today are entirely dependent upon *what you tell yourself about the past and the events of the past.* If you tell yourself you're miserable or helpless because of past events, you are responding to what you are *saying*, not to the *event.*

Tell yourself, *That situation* [whatever it was] *hurt me deeply. I was unhappy and hurt at the time and I still feel bad about it, but now I choose to go on with forgiveness and new happiness in my heart. I choose to see the hope of my future. The Lord Jesus gives me new life each day, and I release myself from the pain of past events.*

*Misbelief guilt* is telling yourself how bad you are even after you've been forgiven. When Jesus forgives you, you are forgiven, *period.* It's important to accept it and to know you are free.

*Godly guilt* is necessary because God uses our consciences to help us change our minds about our misbeliefs and harmful actions. We can then learn the meaning of repentance. We appreciate the glory of fellowship with the Lord Jesus, and we fall in love with Him even more because He forgives us. We know that sin lowers our self-esteem and that doing what is right improves our self-esteem. Many times I pray with people who become convicted of sin when God touches them. This kind of guilt results in something fresh, clean, and beautiful. The person becomes convicted of sin, confesses it, and realizes Jesus took guilt and shame on the cross for our sins and failures.

Sin convicts you and you will experience *godly* guilt feelings. If you don't feel godly guilt over your sin, you may become morose, depressed, and fall into deeper sin. The natural result of sin is guilt, and that guilt can be resolved only by repenting and turning to God. It's impossible for a Christian to live in sin for very long without developing guilt. Denying guilt only makes a person neurotic and miserable.

Sin and guilt keep you from developing the richness of your personality, which can only be discovered in Christ. Guilt restricts you, confines you and your spirit. You become self-directed, self-motivated, self-conscious, and self-possessed. A person who is wrapped up in him/herself makes a very small package. This is neurotic.

The Psalmist prayed that any sin in his heart would be revealed so that he might forsake it. "Search me, O God, and know my heart: try me, and know my thoughts: And see if there be any wicked way in me, and lead me in the way everlasting" (Psalms 139:23).

God delights in mercy, the Word of God tells us (Micah 7:18). He is faithful to forgive us and cleanse us from the ravages of sinful thoughts and behavior (1 John 1:9). He implores us lovingly: "Let the wicked forsake his way, and the unrighteous man his thoughts: and let him return unto the Lord, and he will have mercy upon him; and to our God, for he will abundantly pardon" (Isaiah 55:7).

There is a time in your Christian life when you must take yourself by the scruff of the neck and say, '' (your name) , in the name of Jesus listen to the voice of the Lord. You are a child of the living God and He wants to show you that He is your stronghold. He wants you to know He is your rock and your salvation.''

Make your own sentences to yourself now. This is your Staying Happy strategy coming alive. You tell yourself, ''Get up! The Word of God is yours and it's filled with power. Your ability lies in Jesus Christ and His word. Take Him, (your name) !''

It's exciting to come against the words ''Nobody loves me.'' Those words mean absolutely nothing in the light of *Rejoice evermore* (1 Thessalonians 5:16). Jesus said, *Be of good cheer* (John 16:33). David said, *Be glad in the Lord, and rejoice* (Psalms 32:11). *This* is cause for excitement.

Our guilt flies out the window when we climb aboard the wings of forgiveness to freedom with our new Staying Happy skills. Let's look at why you cling to guilt behavior.

## Common Reasons for Feeling Bad

Complete each of the following statements as thoroughly as you can. Think hard and be honest. This is personal, between you and the Lord only. We are not sin and fault hunting. We are responding *positively* by seeking our best potential! These nine statements are keys to unlock thoughts leading to your growth and happiness in Jesus.

1. I read the Word every day because:_____

_____

*To think about:* What is your relationship with the Holy Spirit? Do you allow Him full reign in your life? Do you have dynamic Christian reading material in your home? Do you have beautiful Christian records to listen to? Do you have top teaching tapes to listen to?

2. I have a regular prayer time because: _____

_____

*To think about:* Are you really accepting how precious you are to God? Do you know how loved you are by Him? Tell yourself out loud now, "I am a Loved Person!" Then tell the Lord, "Thank You, Lord Jesus. I believe Your love will sustain and lift me up higher than myself and to greater peace and happiness than I myself can create without You."

3. I hate lying and refuse to lie about: _____

_____

_____

*To think about:* Do you lie often? When do you lie? What don't you want to admit or face about yourself or your life? What do you dislike and not accept about yourself?

4. I know my needs and constructive ways to have them met are:

_____

_____

*To think about:* Do you treasure what you already have? Do you steal love and appreciation from yourself by denying yourself the right to these things? What are your *true* needs according to God's Word? Do you enjoy planning to have your life fulfilled in every way?

5. I will not lose my temper when: _____

_____

_____

*To think about:* Do you direct your anger toward the thing or person you're actually angry about? Or do you just blow up when you feel like it? Are you afraid of your angry feelings? Can you admit anger and pray openly about these feelings?

6. I will not use profane language when: _____

_____

_____

*To think about:* Is your anger bordering on self-destruction? Whom do you wish to hurt? Do you use profanity to strike back? Do you, as a child does, confuse anger with hate and think of them as the same thing?

7. I can face other people's expectations of me which are: _____

_____

_____

*To think about:* Do you fear responsibility? Do you fear commitment? Be honest and tell yourself what is upsetting as well as rewarding about meeting the expectations of others.

8. When my kids are rebellious, I'm to blame if: _____

_____

_____

*To think about:* Are you afraid of their rejection of you? Is that why you're afraid to discipline them? Explain your feelings to yourself. Do you resent or fear conflict?

9. My mother and father aren't ideal parents because: _____

_____

_____

*To think about:* Are you punishing yourself for *their* problems? Do you fear the same will happen to your children? Can you trust yourself to love and be loved? Can you, emotionally speaking, let your parents go and stop paying for their sins?

Do you notice a pattern in your answers? If you lose your temper when you're running late, for example, it may be because you have enforced a demand on yourself that you can't meet and neither can anyone else. Rather than getting angry at your impossible demand, you might kick the dog or yell at a family member. That's misplaced anger. If you find that you're not reading the Word or praying, is it because you don't know how to face God? Are you unaware of the glory and excitement He has in Himself to share with you daily? God is against anything destructive for you.

Guilt is destructive.

Tell yourself out loud, "It is ungodly and unscriptural to harbor the guilt I feel."

Unresolved guilt can make you neurotic. The greatest therapy you will ever receive is to know in the very fiber of your being that God loves you and forgives you. Release the power of God in your life each moment by telling yourself right now out loud: "I release myself from guilt in the name of Jesus!"

There is new hope and joy that soars through you when you accept the work that Jesus did on the cross for you. Allow your heart and mind to fly upward toward peace and leave your guilt where it belongs—at the foot of the cross. You can now risk loving fully.

The prodigal son began his life of sin and once he was enmeshed in it found it nearly impossible to get out. He went to the very bottom of immorality, to the pits of degeneration, before he was finally able to get back to the real world of forgiveness and love.

*Pray with me: Father, in the name of Jesus, I come against every lie of Satan that has held me bound in guilt. I now take Your worth given to me when You took my sins on Yourself and forgave me. I announce to myself and to my world, "Greater is He who is in me than he who is in the world" (see 1 John 4:4).*

*Forgive me, Lord Jesus, for talking negatively, for not forgiving myself, for underestimating Your enormous heart of love, and for speaking wrong words about myself and others.*

*In the name of Jesus, I refuse guilt and every tormenting aspect of it. I thank You, Lord, for forgiving me. I no longer fear the devil and what he can do to me; I no longer fear what any person can do to me because if You are for me who can be against me?*

*Thank You, Lord Jesus, I am free.*

## STAYING HAPPY IN AN UNHAPPY WORLD
## FORGIVENESS EXERCISE FOR OVERCOMING GUILT

Make a quality decision now to drop the guilt that has held you captive. Say out loud, ''Yes, I choose to release myself from the chains of guilt!'' Write it in your journal, and then go on to complete this final Staying Happy exercise.

1. Pray and ask God to reveal to you those people and events which have triggered guilty feelings. After praying complete the following: I forgive _____ for

_____

(Add to the list as necessary. You will be shocked at the people, events, and your past feelings that have held you captive to guilt.)

2. Say out loud: ''I now know I am not an inferior person because bad things have happened to me. Some bad things I now relinquish and stop paying for are: _____

_____

_____

3. I now remove the ''inferior'' label I've worn and replace it with a new label of: _____

4. Here are three reasons for my new label of self-esteem and self-respect.

A. _____

B. _____

C. _____

5. I no longer fear being hurt or rejected because: _____

_____

# EIGHT

## The Perfect Image of Yourself

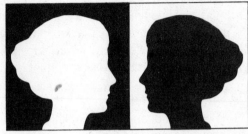

Some of the topics I've covered, such as denial and guilt, are hindrances to a healthy self-image. How we see ourselves is very important to happiness.

### Discovering Self-Discovery

There's a story I like about a quiet and unassertive donkey who happened to have low self-esteem. This donkey felt hopeless about himself, others, and life. One day the woebegone donkey was taking a walk in a field when he found a lion skin which had been left by some hunters. He picked it up, looked at it, and then, because he had nothing else to do, slipped the lion skin over his own body, fitting the lion's head over his own with the mane tumbling around his chest.

About that time some deer came out of the woods and saw the donkey with the lion skin draped over him and thought he was the lion. They froze in fear, then ran into the trees as fast as they could. Soon after that, three rabbits crossed the path and when they saw the donkey in the lion skin they tore off in terror, too.

The donkey felt puffed-up and brave and he decided to amuse himself by trying to roar a bit. He became quite good at it and by the end of the day had successfully frightened nearly every animal in the woods. Then he decided to go to his village and try his new image there. The response was the same. The inhabitants of the village saw him and fled for their lives.

Except one, and that was the fox. He looked at the donkey in the lion skin, who was braying away in pride, and said coolly, "I'm not frightened as the others are. I hear your voice. You're not the lion— you're the donkey!"

The villagers were listening from their hiding places and recognized the lowly donkey. They were furious at him for tricking them. The donkey's owner gave him a sound beating for being so deceitful.

The moral of the story is: Outward appearances may disguise for a while, but the skin that's most important is your own.

## The Labels We Wear

This variation of an Aesop Fable illustrates what a young, promising Christian lawyer told me recently: "I'm really not afraid of the new responsibilities and challenges that are suddenly mine now that I am achieving success, Marie. What I am afraid of is that my inner weaknesses might be discovered and destroy the strong and fearless image people have of me."

The donkey had very little inner security until he found that lion skin. He didn't realize his bravura came from within himself, not from the skin. His poor self-image was converted when he had something to identify with that was strong and brave. We wear our labels in a number of ways. When those labels fall off, there we are with our own skin. It is at this point we must take a good look at ourselves and decide to discover who we are so we're not led by labels only.

My lawyer friend has a self-confident, assertive, and masterful appearance. He has many clients who believe in him. We talked about the difference between appearance and substance. His fears and feelings of unworthiness were out of proportion. He didn't trust the confident and capable lion skin he wore. He told me, "I have a terrible anxiety that people will see how really sensitive I am. I'm not as courageous as I appear, you know. That's only a label they've given me."

Self-discovery means to learn your weaknesses as well as your strengths and accept them. Often we will exalt strong points to such a high degree that we interpret our weak points as embarrassing and threatening. The donkey really had the boldness of the lion in him, but he so concentrated on his weakness and his fears that he never allowed himself to discover other abilities. If he had discovered his abilities to be brave and bray lionlike as *himself* he would have gained acceptance and possibly some admiration from the animals in the woods and village. My friend the lawyer needed to see that instead of hiding and running from his weaknesses, he could accept them as part of his precious self. If he could accept the fact that he had some doubts about his abilities, perhaps they would not be as terrifying to him. But he had to accept *and* admit them. It is not the end of the world to have weaknesses. The devil would like you to believe that you should be without any weaknesses, and if you have any there is something radically the matter with you. What tells you that you're worthless if you have weaknesses?

"Christ in you, the hope of glory" (Colossians 1:27) are the words the Apostle Paul used to tell us about the all-sufficiency of Jesus Christ *in* us. First John 4:8 says God is love. It doesn't say Marie is love or Henry is love or Gloria is love—it says *God is love*. God does the loving in us and through us.

"But the one who joins himself to the Lord is one spirit with Him" (1 Corinthians 6:17 NAS). If it really is true that God is one with you, and if God is love, then you are a person of love. Your feelings of fear, anxiety, nervousness, hatred, self-loathing, and unhappiness do not change this truth. You may feel these negative emotions, but within you your spirit is joined to the Lord.

Jesus prayed in the seventeenth chapter of John's Gospel: "I do not ask in behalf of these alone, but for those also who believe in Me through their word; that they may all be one; even as Thou, Father, art in Me, and I in Thee, that they also may be in Us . . ." (John 17:20, 21 NAS).

Jesus prayed for our self-discovery when He prayed that you and I be one with Him, just like the oneness He knew with His Father. This was a major moment of prayer for the Lord Jesus. God answered Jesus' prayers. When He prayed for you and me, He expected God to answer Him just as He expected God to answer His prayers for the healing of the blind man, the healing of Jairus's daughter, the turning of water into wine, the stilling of the storm, the feeding of the five thousand, and the raising of Lazarus from the dead.

He asked that you and I be *one* with Him—and so we are, if we chose to be. In spite of your human faults, the Holy Spirit who dwells in you is love, making you one with God.

The Apostle Paul said, ''For to me to live is Christ . . .'' (Philippians 1:21). When you discover your real self, you discover the Lord Jesus Christ *within* you. As you now love and live and act, you can say, ''Lord Jesus, You are the one loving and living and acting in my life.''

Before you were a Christian and united with Him as *one,* you were lost in your own humanness without God, even though occasionally you did things that resembled God's personality. A non-Christian isn't necessarily a monster. The difference is, your good deeds and your loveliness of character without God didn't count because your union was wrong. You were behaving in your human strength.

Even the devil himself can appear to be a nice guy. The Apostle Paul wrote to the Christians at Corinth and warned them about false teachers who were putting down the truth of the Gospel and the true messengers of God. He spoke of these men as ''false apostles, deceitful workers, *disguising* themselves as apostles of Christ. And no wonder, for even Satan disguises himself as an angel of light'' (2 Corinthians 11:13, 14 NAS, italics mine).

The Apostle Paul then says, ''Therefore it is not surprising if his servants [Satan's servants] also disguise themselves as servants of righteousness; whose end shall be according to their deeds'' (2 Corinthians 11:15 NAS).

> *Blessed are the ears that hear*
> *the pulse of the Divine whisper,*
> *and give no heed to the many*
> *whisperings of the world.*
> *Thomas a Kempis*

Can you hear when God whispers in your ear? Can you hear when He leads you away from error? The Holy Spirit is the One who convicts you of error. He always guides you in the way of truth. Forgiveness is always the way of truth; even Confucious admitted that when he said, ''To be wronged or robbed is nothing unless you continue to remember it.'' An important army general once said to John Wesley, ''I never forgive and I never forget,'' and John Wesley answered, ''Then sir, I hope you never sin.''

The Holy Spirit knows that He is the one who can produce in you that which pleases God. Christ is our life and living this life means Christ living in you. When God gave Moses the Law, He said, in effect, "Take this law to the people to show them what I am like, and if they will keep this law, they will be like me. I will be their God and they will be my people." Of course, the people couldn't follow the laws of God perfectly. The laws were *the character of God* and they couldn't follow without the character of God *within*. You and I, because we are Christians, because we have said yes to Jesus Christ, because we have asked Him to fill us with His Holy Spirit, *have* the character of God within us. Now you have the ability to live as the Apostle Paul said, "For it is God who is at work *in* you, both to will and to work for His good pleasure" (Philippians 2:13 NAS, italics mine).

God now lives His life through you. A new person has been brought into being within you because you now have a new heart. Many people who have been Christians for years are still trying to live as the Jews did in Moses' day, struggling to be good and do good, and always falling short. He promised that His people would have a new heart, and that the Law would be written not on tablets of stone but on fleshly tablets of the heart. You are not a bad person striving to be a good person. You are a good person—you are the righteousness of God in Christ. You are a new creature. See yourself in your true identity. The discovery of who you really are can be like the spreading dawn in the deepest recesses of your being. Your permanent identity is Jesus Christ. "Therefore if any man be in Christ, he is a new creature: old things are passed away; behold all things are become new" (2 Corinthians 5:17).

## How Do I Accept My Failures and Shortcomings?

When you are one with the Lord Jesus, you discover your real self. When you don't do things that look like Him, when you slip up and commit a sin, you are not condemned. The glorious union you have with the Lord Jesus gives you the wherewithal and right to confess your sin, acknowledge that it is covered by the blood of Jesus Christ, accept your forgiveness, and go on with the business of living victoriously. Think of your sins as you would a blemish—a blemish needing to be washed, cleansed, medicated, and healed. Charles L.

Allen wrote in *The Touch of the Master's Hand,* "Forgiveness is the cloak for your naked, sinful souls." The Psalmist said, "Blessed is he whose transgression is forgiven, whose sin is covered" (Psalms 32:1). God covers our sins with Himself and His forgiveness. He cleanses, washes, heals, renews, and makes clean again that which has been wounded and angry at God. The blemishes on our souls are removed because "he is faithful and just to forgive us our sins, and to cleanse us from all unrighteousness" (1 John 1:9).

## What You Tell Yourself About Yourself

Differentiate now between what you were and acted like yesterday and what you are and can act like today. You are the righteousness of God (2 Corinthians 5:21), and when something appears imperfect in your thoughts, when you sink into doubt and despair, choose to hear the truth as God tells it to you. When you realize what I have been saying about change throughout this book, you will be able to see that this change takes place in your attitude of acceptance. God is constantly revealing the flawless, magnificent character of Jesus Christ *in* you. In order to discover your real self, you realize God is living out His life in you. The changes you make are all directly related to the degree with which you have fought this truth. Change can be stressful because it calls upon you to adapt, and any adaptation stresses your body systems. Being afraid to change hinders your happiness. Fear is the one emotion which dooms you to repeat your mistakes of the past.

We cannot move on in our personal growth if we try to leave conflicts and unresolved situations behind. John Wood said in *What Are You Afraid Of?,* "Because we have been hurt we will carry it with us, afraid to be hurt again, and live out the self-defeating patterns our fear of pain sets up." In order to be happy, it is necessary to face what it is we're afraid of.

You have the power to accept or reject the truth as Jesus has revealed it to you. You may *desire* to change from the old way of negative, hurting behaviors to the new and healthy, fulfilled life in Christ, but perhaps you haven't yet stepped into realizing what you have in Christ and who you are in Him. He is the Real You in you. The Spirit of truth now leads you just as once the "spirit of error" led you. The only victory is in walking in the power of the Holy Spirit, because "As he is, so are we in this world" (1 John 4:17).

Jesus led His life on earth conscious only of His Father in all things. In everything He did and every person whose life He touched, He was conscious of His Father's mind and heart toward all. You can be as conscious of Jesus in all things as He was His Father. Settle in your mind and heart now that your identity, your true self, is Jesus Christ Himself in you.

## The Joy of Avoiding Burnout

One definition of burnout is when our physical and mental resources are exhausted—when we are worn out by excessively striving to reach some unrealistic expectation imposed by ourselves or the values of society. It's a condition when we are depleted. Being one with Jesus Christ gives us the power to fight back and become our real selves. Usually when we burn out, it's because we step outside of the reality of ourselves with Christ in us.

There was a young man named Wally who did not go into the priesthood as his mother so earnestly desired him to do. Wally became a tireless do-gooder, to the point of being nonassertive and somewhat like a doormat in the great hallway of life. He excused his behavior by putting a religious label on himself: "a humble person who loves to do unto others." He said all he wanted was to be a cheerful giver and help people. But the truth was, he wasn't trying to please God with all his giving and goodwill. It wasn't God living His life through him and expressing Himself. It was Wally's human nature trying to be religious. It wore him out because it's frustrating to try to give happiness to an unreceptive, unhappy world. Wally burned out and became bitterly dejected. He felt broken and hurt, with tormenting feelings of alienation and hopelessness. Wally had to learn that it wasn't God he was trying to please, it was his mother.

Whom are you trying to please? You will become a slave to that one. What labels are you wearing? When your heart is set on God, filled with Him, you and He become forever one. That's the true discovery of your true self.

## Staying happy Key I*

**God is constantly revealing the loving, joyful character of Jesus Christ in you.**

### STAYING HAPPY IN AN UNHAPPY WORLD
### PERFECT IMAGE EXERCISE

**1.** Whom do you want to please most of all in the world?
_____
List godly ways of pleasing a person. _____
**2.** Write down three of the most common things you tell yourself
about yourself. _____
_____
_____

Are they the same words your loving, heavenly Father says about
you?
**3.** Name three attributes of Jesus that you express in your life now.
_____
_____
_____

# NINE

# How Do Others See You?

Carolyn came to me devastated in all respects. She began to cry before she sat down and blurted how badly she was hurting. "You can't believe what a fool I've been!" she sobbed with tears running down her face. "I never dreamed I could fall into sin like this. I don't know what's the matter with me. How could I commit such a terrible sin? Oh, what is wrong with me?"

Carolyn and her husband ran a youth establishment and ministered to the young people of the streets. She had committed a sin for which she could not forgive herself. *She saw the sin and herself as one.* I explained this in the chapter on guilt, and here is another example of the importance of differentiating *what you do* from *who you are.* In the earlier chapter on the work fanatic, we talked about our work not being our personhood. We are not secretary, author, speaker, bricklayer, or whatever we do. We are children of God first and foremost.

We respond to life as Christians, not as victims of sin and doom. Because you are God's person you have the ability to follow His leading and not confuse what you do with who you are. This applies to sin. Because you committed a sin you are not one with that sin. You already know that you are a sinner because you are a human being. However, the sin you have committed is *not* your identity.

## Do You See Yourself as a Whole Person?

God wants you to be free to be yourself. If His spirit lives in you, "yourself" is infused with Himself. God defines you and me by Himself, His standards, and His character. As a Christian, your identity and wholeness is in Jesus Christ. You want to be like Jesus because He is true wholeness. In Him you become whole, too.

There is also a difference between what you want and who you are. Carolyn wanted to live the Christian life. She wanted to be like Jesus. When she committed the sin she felt so wretched about, she was not thinking of her oneness with Jesus; in fact, she was responding directly to the alluring drawing power of the devil. She responded to his alluring power in her human nature, not in her God nature. That was why she felt so bad about it later.

## Creating Your Behaviors

I'll never forget a couple named Debbie and Alan who sat in my office wanting to vent their anger at one another, with me as their witness. This is not unusual in family counseling. I wouldn't let them begin their fight and insisted they say good things about each other, but the husband managed to get in a barb when he said to his wife, "You're the president of your ladies' Bible club. You're such a happy and friendly person when you're with them and everybody loves you. They should only know what the *real* you is like."

"That's interesting!" I interjected. "Does that mean that Debbie is only her real self when she's negative or behaving badly?"

Alan was sullen. Debbie said, appropriately, "Well, I should be able to express myself at home, shouldn't I?"

Debbie thought "expressing herself" meant to have the right to vent her anger and engage in outbursts of temper and faultfinding. Her husband sneered. "You do a lot of that *expressing* stuff."

Now I addressed Alan directly. "In your words, Alan, tell me what your wife is like when she's leading the Bible study or when she is in her leadership capacity with the ladies in her Christian organization."

He didn't hesitate. "She's friendly, nice; she smiles a lot, acts loving and really caring. I've seen her be a lot more understanding to someone she doesn't even know than she is to her family. Her attitude is the difference between night and day."

I could hear the hurt in his voice as he spoke. I asked him, "Do you wonder if she cares as much about you as she does about the ladies in her group?"

His voice lowered. He spoke slowly. "It just seems she gives them so much of herself. But for me, she's mostly, I don't know. . . ." It was difficult for him to describe his hurt, which he had expressed only in anger before. He was honestly confronting his hurt now.

Debbie needed to recognize his openness and listen to him with an open heart. As he spoke I could see her soften somewhat.

"I guess I have been short-tempered and unkind at home," she admitted to Alan, "but I really think it's because I'm overworked. You don't help me. . . ." She didn't utter this last accusation with conviction. She saw that she was making excuses.

Debbie needed to see that (1) her behavior and she were not one and the same, and (2) she had within her the ability to be as kind and as accepting at home with her husband as she was with the ladies in her group.

She could be the same cheerful, outgoing person under careful scrutiny of others as when alone with her family. It is not true that we are bunches of personalities all rolled up in one package, to pull out according to the situation at hand. That would make us victims of circumstances.

You can be in control of the way you behave *at all times*. It is disturbing to me when we lose part of our personhood because of a situation.

Debbie tried very hard to defend her behavior by telling me how unpleasant and unhelpful Alan was at home, and that was why she couldn't be as accepting as she would like to be. She wanted to defend herself by denying that *she* was responsible for her behavior. She didn't understand it was possible to be pleasant even when things weren't going the way she wanted them to.

Debbie was practically paralyzed with negative lies. Notice the web she spun around herself: First, she did not confront Alan openly and directly with her feelings by telling him something such as, "Alan, I am hurting because when you don't help me as I think you should, I feel you don't care about me and how overworked I am. Is this the message you want me to receive?" Alan would then have the opportunity to respond honestly and openly with his feelings.

Second, Debbie didn't realize she could be the same cheerful, giving person she was in public in the laundry room or the kitchen or the supermarket. It is a choice. Debbie tried to defend her poor behavior by telling herself that her husband didn't deserve her kindness. She tried to tell herself that Alan hadn't *earned* his right to have a cheerful wife. She tried to tell herself that he was the one to blame because he made it so unpleasant for her at home.

Have you ever been kind to a stranger? Have you ever smiled at someone you didn't know? If we can be nice to strangers, kind to people who are not involved in our personal lives, we can be kind to *all*, and that includes our families. That same skill, to be pleasant even when we don't know the history of a person, is there when we do know the history of a person. You don't ask a stranger to prove his credentials before you smile at him, do you?

## Your Feelings

"But I don't *feel* like being nice when I get home. I just don't *feel* like talking or being pleasant," Debbie told me.

But feelings change. A feeling isn't forever. This wife *chose* not to be pleasant or cheerful. If you feel sullen or quiet or as though you will never laugh again, understand that these are *feelings* and only feelings. Feelings always change.

These questions, "Is it all right if I don't feel like talking?" and "Is it all right if I am unfriendly at times?" are acceptable if they are not excuses for poor behavior. Many times we excuse plain, old rudeness by claiming we're "tired" or we'll excuse our neglect and cruelty with explanations like, "I don't feel well."

A Harvard University dean once told a student who hadn't completed an assignment, "You'll find, young man, that most of the work of the world is done by people who aren't feeling very well one way or the other."

Debbie learned how to function when she didn't feel well one way or the other. She *did* change. She was a beautiful woman with modellike features and she had gotten away with being unpleasant because her beauty had carried her through. The Lord would not put up with that, however. He demands inner beauty first.

Alan changed, too. We change when we allow the Holy Spirit to work in our lives and teach us that we can be lovely in all situations, and that we do not have to earn the right to someone else's kindness.

Alan and Debbie dropped many of their defenses and discovered they could trust each other with their deep feelings and longings for love. Change did not come easy and they had to work at it. Like many other people, they first had to accept their need for change and not be ashamed or defensive. My friend Sue Townsend once said something I'll long remember: "The unchanging God keeps *us* in change."

Get in touch with your feelings; acquire the skill of creating something wonderful with your thoughts every day. You can think about God's Word every single day, and when you do, your mind will enlarge and you will begin to think *God's thoughts!* You begin to see and experience:

| | |
|---|---|
| Possibilities | *Not* hopelessness |
| Joy | *Not* desperation |
| Contentment | *Not* anxiety |
| Peace | *Not* rage |
| Acceptance | *Not* envy |
| Self-esteem | *Not* pride |
| Integrity | *Not* loneliness |
| Fulfillment | *Not* fear |

I believe you can teach yourself to feel good about yourself. Don't confuse feeling good about yourself with being popular. Popularity means that *other* people feel good about you. What you think about yourself, your character, and your own accomplishments is worth taking time to determine.

John Greenleaf Whittier said in his poem *Andrew Rykman's Prayer,* "Let me be the thing I meant. . . ." I am convinced that you can change without spending years and a lot of money to get to the point where your life is new and you have developed new living habits. I believe that if you employ the keys I am sharing with you here, you can experience a new sweep of the Holy Spirit in your mind and emotions, and you *will* change. You can be the thing you meant and find peace that, as Whittier says, is "dearer than joy until things sweet and good seem [your] natural habitude." Archbishop Trench wrote these words:

> *Lord, what a change within us one short hour*
> *Spent in Thy Presence will prevail to make!*

## How Do You See Yourself?

Check below the attributes which best describe you:

| | |
|---|---|
| Fun _____ | Giving_____ |
| Intelligent _____ | Wise _____ |
| Unprejudiced _____ | Forgiving _____ |
| Enterprising _____ | Strong _____ |
| Loyal _____ | Loving _____ |
| Happy _____ | Hardworking _____ |
| Honest _____ | Patient _____ |
| Gentle _____ | Thoughtful _____ |
| Disciplined _____ | Fair and just _____ |
| Energetic _____ | Attractive _____ |
| Creative _____ | |

Now go over the same list and check how many of the above your best friend would agree with. Take your time and think about what you are doing. Don't take this lightly just because these happen to be positive attributes. Does your best friend really consider you thoughtful? How attractive does your best friend think you are?

When you are finished checking the attributes your best friend would, go over the same list and check those that your husband or wife would check. How does your spouse see you? Be very honest. How many of the above would your spouse say describe you?

Next, go over the list and check which descriptions your mother or father would agree with. This is very important. As you go over these descriptions, notice the difference among reactions toward you.

Last, go over the above list and check with descriptions your children would check (if you have children).

Add the checks you made for yourself and total them. Next add the checks of your best friend and total them. Follow with the checks of your parents, spouse, and children. Total those. Which of these people in your life see you as most positive? The answer should tell you something about yourself as well as your relationships. After you have done this, go over the same list and check the descriptions your boss at work would agree with.

The descriptions you uncover will provide new ideas because possibly you have never really thought of how other people see you. It was a revelation to a friend of mine when she realized people tend to think the same way about us as we think about ourselves. She told me people didn't see her as creative. I asked her, "Do you see yourself as creative?" She sighed and said, "I have always admired creative people and I have always longed to be a creative person, but I really don't see myself as creative." Neither did anybody else. The ideas we project about ourselves are important because others will agree with you.

Sometimes other people's outstanding attributes intimidate us and we put limitations on the way we think about ourselves. A five-year-old child will not consider himself a good artist when he compares his crayon drawings with the professional drawings of his artist uncle. My friend didn't consider herself creative because she didn't excel in any particular talent she considered worthwhile. She thought talent meant being a musician, artist, writer, or performer. She never considered herself a talented housekeeper or mother. In fact, when I suggested that, she laughed as though I had said something funny.

"Oh, Marie, must you *always* be positive?"

"But I'm being honest," I protested. "I consider you very talented. You run your household with flair and imagination and it's an inspiration to me and to many other people. I love the way you give a luncheon in your home and I love the way you've decorated the house. You have creativity in your everyday life and I admire you for that."

She was giggling now and finally said, "I never thought housekeeping and having friends in for lunch was necessarily creative."

"Maybe the activities in themselves aren't," I answered. *"It's the way you do them."*

On the day of his death at the age of seventy-eight, artist Pierre Renoir painted some flowers and then said, "I think I am beginning to understand something about it. . . . Today I learned something."

## Becoming More Creative

Life is what happens to you while you are planning your future, I've heard said, and it is true, isn't it? My question is, what quality of life are we living? The poet Ralph Waldo Emerson said, "A weed is a plant whose virtues have not been discovered." I believe a truly creative person is one who knows how to make something big out of something small, something happy out of something sad, something funny out of pain, something sweet out of something bitter, and something good out of bad. If beauty is in the eye of the beholder, so is ugliness.

I have known many talented people in the arts who were very unhappy in their personal lives. Many successful people are not personally successful. A person who is an achiever in one area of life can mistakenly be expected by others to be an achiever in *every* area, including his or her personal life. This is not necessarily true. We need personal creativity—the creative ability to turn hurts to joyful prayers. Ralph Barton was a caricature artist who was famous in the 1920s. He was heralded as one of the most original minds of his generation. He pinned this note to his pillow before he took his life: ''I have had few difficulties, many friends, great successes; I have gone from wife to wife, and from house to house, visited great countries of the world, but I am fed up with inventing devices to fill up twenty-four hours a day.''

Here was a man who had a great talent in one area of his life, but his personal life was tragically bereft. Many people remain unfulfilled, nonspiritual children their whole lives through sliding along on their ''talent'' for happiness and a sense of belonging. Then the realization occurs that something is missing and there is a horrible sense of emptiness and panic. Henry David Thoreau said, ''Most men live lives of quiet desperation,'' and if that's true, it's a sad commentary on human ability. I don't buy it, not for a minute! It is true that many people idolize human creativity and talent. They don't realize true creativity is reaching into the vistas of heaven through Jesus Christ, and in the power of the Holy Spirit to take the greatest talent and creativity there ever was or will be in a God-filled life.

The poet Byron, a talented man, said these tragic words: ''My days are in the yellow leaf, the flowers and the fruits of life are gone and the worm and the canker, and the grief are mine alone.'' Another creative man, H. G. Wells, the famous historian and philosopher, said at the age of sixty-one, ''I have no peace. All life is at the end of its tether.''

Who defines our personalities and talents? Do others make our decisions for us or do we?

## Defining Who We Are

It is the poorer person who believes that other people define who he is. On the self-discovery questionnaire I sent out, I asked the question "What do you think is the greatest achievement you have made in your life?" The answers received were marvelously diverse. I was very excited to see that most of the answers showed personal achievements such as, "Facing my fears and taking steps to change." Some people answered, "Accepting Jesus as my Savior." Many people left it blank. What is your greatest achievement? Could you answer yes to any of the following?

1. I consider it an achievement that I can create something good out of what looks impossibly difficult. _____

2. I consider it an achievement that I can create a pleasant atmosphere when it is in turmoil. _____

3. I consider it an achievement that I can create an atmosphere of abundance even when it looks as if I have nothing. _____

4. I consider it an achievement that I can create a feeling of acceptance and warmth toward the people around me, even if I do not totally approve of them. _____

Another question I asked on the self-discovery questionnaire was, "If you could be anyone in the whole world, who would it be?" I was surprised at the answers. Many people told me they would like to be a certain Christian personality, but 97 percent of the people surveyed said they just wanted to be *themselves.*

If you could have any job or position you wanted, what would it be? If you were to change anything in your life, what would it be? Every person I surveyed wanted to change something in his or her life. Many answered they would like different jobs or positions. Several told me they wanted the very job they already had. What puzzled me was the answer "I just want to be a better person."

I don't understand what a "better person" means. If you were to ask a friend who is very close to you whether you should be a better person or not, what would he or she say? If you asked the same friend *how* you could be a better person, what would be the answer?

I asked a group of teenage girls this question and they laughed at the idea. Then one by one they were instructed to tell each other how they should change. They laughed so hard it was difficult for them to say anything, let alone some critical or constructive bit of advice. One girl, between guffaws, told the friend on her right, "I think you should change that beautiful sweater you're wearing and give it to me."

"Wait a minute," I interrupted. "Do you think she dresses better than someone else?" The giggling stopped. Another girl spoke up. "Sometimes people make you feel bad when you look good," she said. It got quieter in the room. One of the girls asked, "What's wrong with trying to look good?"

Another said, "Some people are always competing."

They were able to express some valuable thoughts to one another about jealousy and competition. The girls were open with each other and admitted they would like to have things different. They each expressed a need for acceptance at school and for the freedom to change and improve for the better in a number of areas.

At the close of the discussion, a girl in the back of the room offered this observation: "I think to be a better person means to be more accepting of other people."

Then a quiet, soft-faced girl near me who had hardly said a word all afternoon spoke up and summed up every girl's feelings as honestly as I've ever heard: "I think if I were more accepting of *myself* I wouldn't have to compete with anyone else."

How do we see one another? We see one another by the way we project ourselves.

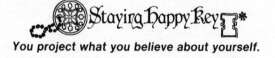

## Staying Happy Key *

**You project what you believe about yourself.**

I like this story about a little girl who was drawing with her crayons. Her mother asked her what her subject was and the little girl answered, "I'm drawing God." The mother protested, "But nobody knows what God looks like." The child kept drawing and then said firmly, "They'll know when I'm finished."

Staying happy in an unhappy world means you must bring something of *you* into your world. Without your gifts and special beauty, the world is an unhappier place. God wants you to reach levels of fulfillment and confidence beyond your natural capabilities. Your world needs your creativity. Lack of confidence steals creativity from you. Here are some other creativity thieves:

>Perfectionism
>
>Timidity (shyness is *not* a virtue!)
>
>Sticking to old habits
>
>Discouragement
>
>Inability to be alone
>
>Fear of failure
>
>Denial and dishonesty

A woman who was approaching her fifty-fifth birthday came up to me after I had spoken at a mother-daughter banquet. "Marie, your message was so good for the young people," she said. I caught the unspoken self-sorrow in the tone of her voice. "And what about you?" I asked, smiling at her. "Was the message for *you,* too?"

"Well, I don't know if I can be all those things you talked about," she answered timidly. "I'm so *old.* I'm too old to be creative."

"What?" I responded incredulously. "It's a good thing Michelangelo didn't think like you do—and it's a good thing Sophocles, Goethe, Tennyson, Verdi, or Haydn didn't think like you do either, for that matter. They all created far into old age. What a poorer world we would have without their gifts to us."

"But isn't fifty-five *old?*" she asked.

"Nobody ever told Verdi he was too old when he composed *Falstaff* at the age of eighty. And nobody told Titian he was too old when he painted his famous *Battle of Lepanto* at the age of ninety-eight and then lived to be one hundred. Nobody told Corrie ten Boom she was too old when she was still traveling the world speaking for Jesus at the age of eighty. Nobody told Sally Conlin she was too old at the age of sixty-five when she started her ministry for wayward girls and opened a halfway house in the slums of Minneapolis, which she ran and directed.

Emerson wrote these words:

> *Though we travel the world over*
> *to find the beautiful,*
> *We must carry it with us*
> *or we find it not.*

The Holy Spirit is creative and you have the Holy Spirit within you so that you can recognize the power and potential you have in Him at any age. Promise yourself now that you will no longer put yourself down by putting down your creativity. I love these words of the renowned musician Pablo Casals: "I am thankful to think that at my age I can work on things that are worthwhile. I am almost ninety . . . imagine! At my age I can still do exactly as I did when I was young. I know that I am a happy man." At the age of ninety Casals could still have time to play, conduct, compose, travel, and enjoy life the way he had as a young man. He applied his creativity not only to his music but to all areas of his life.

Alex Osborn, author of *Applied Imagination,* believes creativity is a teachable, learnable art. He believes that instead of trying to think critically and imaginatively at the same time, we should use our critical mind at one time and our creative mind at another.

## What Does It Take to Be Creative?

Silvano Arieti, author of *Creativity: The Magic Synthesis,* gives eight one-word conditions for creativity. I've listed them here, followed by my comments.

*Aloneness.* "Original ideas do not happen in groups." Communication with God means to be alone with Him—where creativity in your life is rooted.

*Inactivity.* "If a person must always fix his attention on external work, he limits the possibility of developing his inner resources." We must take time to rest our souls in His care, His love, His spirit.

*Daydreaming.* "Not solely autobiographical, but a source of fantasy to open up new realms of growth and discovery." This is a time to think about heaven and reflect on its glory.

*Free thinking.* "When a person allows his mind to wander without restraints or organization." I believe this is the state of mind where praise takes place. We praise the Lord with abandon and freedom as our minds concentrate joyfully on praise thoughts. We express praise words without restraint and worship happily and gleefully.

*Direct analogy.* Like Alexander Graham Bell, who compared the human ear to a machine which became the telephone, the Christian compares himself with Christ and identifies with Him completely in all aspects of life and being.

*Gullibility.* "A willingness to explore everything: to be open, innocent, and naive." The word *vulnerable* is fitting for the Christian. It's when we are completely open to the work of God in our lives.

*Remembrance of past conflicts.* "Forgetting early trauma and conflicts may require a voluntary act of mental suppression." We must remember that conflicts *always* exist in the psyche of man. What is most important is the ability to transform them into something creative. God never intended us to be robots without feelings. The most inspiring Christian works have been wrought through conflict.

*Discipline.* "Many would-be creative persons are reluctant to submit themselves to the rigor of learning techniques and practicing discipline and logical thinking. . . . They ignore the fact that even such people as Giotto, Leonardo, Freud, and Einstein had teachers."

I've commented on Arieti's conditions for creativity because I think Christians can be the most creative people in the world. Arieti claims that without commitment to action, creativity may never emerge in a person. I'm surprised at the number of Christians who are unable to sustain commitment. They're involved but not committed. In fact, many can't even give appropriate definitions of the words *involvement* and *commitment.* The best I've heard is humorously to the point. The Reverend Robert Ard, president of the Black Leadership Council, explained the difference between involvement and commitment this way: "When you look at a plate of ham and eggs, you know the chicken was involved, but the pig was committed."

## Your Surroundings Influence Your Creativity

Psychologist Abraham Maslow believed that creative people are self-actualizing persons, and that in order to promote creativity there must be a climate for creativity. I agree with Maslow, but as a Christian, not a humanist. The Holy Spirit gives us the very mind of Christ to think with open minds and clear heads and with a sense of wonder. This does not necessarily mean we have to be smart to be creative.

E. P. Torrance, author of *Guiding Creative Talent,* stresses that creativity requires both sensitivity and independence. Torrance lists some characteristics of the creative person, eighty-four in all. He lists them alphabetically from "Accepts disorder" to "Withdrawn." He describes a highly creative person as "altruistic, energetic, industrious, persistent, self-assertive, and versatile." Notice that on this list there is nothing about being intelligent. A high IQ will not impair your creativity, but fear of someone's opinion of you will.

Jim Bakker, PTL president, once said, "Riches don't make a person successful. Ideas do. You can have an idea and be rich." Mary Henle wrote in an article titled, "The Birth and Death of Ideas," quoted in Silvano Arieti's *Creativity: The Magic Synthesis,* that the first requisite for creative thinking is receptivity. She wrote, "We cannot get creative ideas by searching for them; but if we are not receptive to them, they will not come." Henle asserts that creativity requires a certain attitude on our part which involves "detaching oneself from one's ongoing concerns and without particular expectations, heeding the ideas that come."

## When Are You Most Creative?

For many people the most creative time in their lives is when they are children. The child is usually creative and curious, filled with the desire to explore and learn. Dr. Thomas A. Harris, proponent of transactional analysis and author of *I'm OK–You're OK,* describes the child "within us" as the one with "urges to touch and feel and experience, and where the recordings of the glorious pristine feelings of first discoveries lie. In the child are recorded the countless, grand *a-ha* experiences, the firsts in the life of the small person, the first drinking from the garden hose, the first stroking of the soft kitten, the first sure hold on a mother's nipple, the first time the lights go on in response to his flicking the switch, the first submarine chase of the bar of soap, the repetitious going back to do these glorious things again and again."

When you feel happy, without the burden of the world on your shoulders, your mind is free to think new thoughts, new solutions, new ideas. Your creativity lies in how close your relationship is to God. God gives us the words "Fret not" because He knows that fretting can bottle up our wondrous personalities like nothing else will. "Let not your heart be troubled, neither let it be afraid. . . . Ye believe in God, believe also in me" (John 14:27, 1).

A student of mine told me this amazing experience: "Just this morning I suddenly remembered another morning when I was much younger. It was as though I were a child again and it was time to get ready for school. I went to my little brother's room to wake him. He had just awakened and was sitting on the edge of his bed. He wasn't looking at anything, really, he was just sort of waking up and staring softly out through his clear green eyes. His gentle face and the warmth of the moment was like a sudden break in time, I remember. I stood in the doorway of his room and said, 'What are you thinking about, Billy?' He looked up at me and grinned somewhat sleepily and said, 'I don't know.' That moment has remained in my mind all these years. His sweet boy face, his room, his stillness—he silenced the rush and the anxious race of morning just by *being.*"

Her gaze dropped and she said, "I think I've really lost something very precious in life. I don't have moments like that now. If I saw one of my children staring into space first thing in the morning I'd holler and yell that they'd miss the school bus if they didn't hurry up. I realize how hassled and unquiet my life is now. That morning was so long ago when my little brother sat on the edge of the bed, just sitting in the freshness and sweetness of our mornings. He was so young and life was so hopeful—then."

My student longed for creativity to return to her life—some daydreaming! Life had become mundane and fraught with pressures and demands. Her own children meant responsibility to her, unlike the friend her little brother had been.

Too many of us live hardworking lives without relief. We even play as though we're at work. A musician friend of mine with a genius IQ can do almost anything, and everything he does, he does well. He attacks life instead of allowing life to happen to him. If he plays tennis, he plays it as though he were competing for an Olympic medal. He is also a creative person and I pray for him regularly. I pray he'll always be able to smell the roses and watch a sunset without thinking of ways to market these experiences.

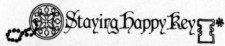

**I am creative because I am linked to the creative power of God by the Holy Spirit within me.**

### Your Creative Self Deserves Creative Expression

What do you do when you're alone? Please take time to answer this. Observe yourself in your alone hours and write down the way you spend your time and the activities you create for yourself. Do you watch television? Do you read? Do you get on the phone and talk to somebody? Do you cook, clean, write, run, walk, daydream, sleep, study, pray? Take note every day of those alone hours. We must spend a certain portion of our lives alone and since we do, it is important that those hours be blessed. Have you blessed your alone hours?

Say with me now:

*Lord Jesus, bless my alone hours that they be full and rich and that my mind be creative so that my thoughts create good out of seemingly bad and so I can become in my heart and actions more than I can imagine. Bless me indeed, Lord Jesus. Amen.*

### Know Who You Are

Jesus knew who He was. He knew His position of authority and He knew the power that was within Him. He knew that His life was a life more than blessed. He knew when He prayed things would happen. Even at the grave of Lazarus He did not falter or quake at the threat of defeat. The creative mind of God was within Him, just as the creative mind of God is within *you*. Jesus didn't doubt this when He prayed loud and clear at the tomb of Lazarus:

*Father, I thank thee that thou hast heard me. And I knew that thou hearest me always: but because of the people which stand by I said it, that they may believe that thou hast sent me. And when he thus had spoken, he cried with a loud voice, Lazarus, come forth.*

*John 11:41–43*

The Lord Jesus is saying to *you* right now, " (your name) , come forth!''

## STAYING HAPPY IN AN UNHAPPY WORLD
## SELF-IMAGE EXERCISE

Do I give myself the right to be myself? _____

Do I give myself the right to accept my past? _____

Do I give myself the right to enjoy life even though I'm not as perfect as I would like to be? _____

Do I give myself the right to say ''I'm okay'' even though when I look around I see other people whom I think are much more okay than me? _____

Do I give myself the right to love myself even when I don't have a goal? _____

Do I give myself the right to be a worthwhile and giving person even though other people seem to be more giving and sacrificial than I? _____

Do I give myself the right to be considered intelligent even though I haven't had as much schooling as some other people? _____

Do I give myself the right to stop making excuses for my shortcomings? _____

Do I give myself the right to accept mercy and compassion because I deserve it? _____

Do I give myself the right to open my heart to hear the loving words of God and to feel His heart's arms around me, holding me and telling me, ''I have loved thee with an everlasting love: therefore with lovingkindness have I drawn thee'' (Jeremiah 31:3)?

_____

# TEN

# The Staying Happy in an Unhappy World Recovery Plan

## The Blues, the Blahs, and Burnout No More

How much thought and effort do you give to the truth that you are a unique and valuable human being? Usually the thing we consider most unique or valuable about ourselves is our suffering and our amazing capacity for pain. I've never met anyone who didn't consider his or her suffering immensely important. What value do we give to our ability to be *happy*? Usually when we are hurting or when we have hurt, we feel nobody else could possibly suffer as badly. We seem enormously important at these times because the hurt is of such large proportion.

Think of a time when you've felt depressed. At that time it was difficult for you to consider anyone else's depression or negative feelings as crucial or worse than yours. When you have felt anxious or nervous in the past, you know your energy was not spent helping someone else's anxiety and nervousness at that time. If you are a victim of burnout or in the throes of falling apart, your uppermost thoughts are directed at you, not at another hurting person.

You're important, and not only when your feelings are extreme on one side or the other of happiness. A difference between happy and unhappy is that when you feel unhappy, you are concerned mainly with yourself, excluding all else. When you feel happy you want to share your feelings. You become giving and helpful and your feelings of happiness produce more happiness.

If you have suffered and if you suffer now in your life, it is not a sin to admit it. You are not more or less important at these difficult times than at other times. Your illnesses, serious operations, accidents, and hospitalizations are important experiences, but because they are traumatic, they don't make you more important than when you're happy and feeling good. Novelist Aldous Huxley said, "Experience is not what happens to you; it is what you do with what happens to you." If you have hurt, it is important to know how to fight back for your *Staying Happy in an Unhappy World* privileges. You are more important than your problems and your successes. *You* count in spite of your positive or negative feelings.

According to the National Institute of Mental Health, each year about 15 million Americans suffer from depression and receive treatment. Then there are the countless people who feel depressed and never see a doctor for the condition. Worry, fear, depression, and intense self-concern is self-destructive mental activity. Voltaire said, "The longer we dwell on our misfortunes, the greater is their power to harm us."

Tell yourself, as Dr. Hans Selye advises in his book *Stress Without Distress*, that stress is "the spice of life." Tell yourself the truth which writer James Baldwin knew: "Not everything that is faced can be changed, but nothing can be changed until it is faced." Dr. Selye says that motivation is essential. I believe you can suffer many pains and indignities as a Christian when your motivation stays intact.

If you are really motivated to know God, to love Him, and to please Him, you will be able to say to yourself and the emotional suffering you have experienced, "It is no longer I who lives, but Christ within me." A major struggle we face when we are fighting against emotional problems is the struggle between choosing God and choosing our own disastrous human nature behaviors. You are valuable to God. You are His asset no matter what else you may have thought to be true.

*"My beloved is mine, and I am his;*
*'For behold, the winter is past,*
*The rain is over and gone. . . .*
*'The fig tree has ripened its figs,*
*And the vines in blossom have*
*        given forth their fragrance.*
*Arise, my darling, my beautiful one,*
*And come along!"*
            Song of Songs 2:16, 11, 13 NAS

## Qualifications for Okayness

Do you think a person has to qualify to be worthwhile? Do you have a realistic understanding of your own worthwhile self? There are many restrictions we place on ourselves and one of them is how we *look*. The eating-disordered person, for instance, from the obese to the anorectic and bulimic believes, *"Control* makes me worthwhile." To this person control is all-important. A person is not entitled to self-respect without it. To the dieting fanatic nothing he or she ever does has real meaning or value unless he or she is thin. Many people believe that irresponsibility and fat go together, so if a person is fat it follows that person is not worthwhile. What do you see as worthwhile? Do you have certain taboos or restrictions, too?

I interviewed many famous Christian leaders as I was writing this book and I was surprised to learn that nearly every one of them felt, at one time, as though they were utter failures in life and certainly not candidates for feeling worthwhile. Charles Swindoll told me, "When I first started in the ministry, it seemed as though it was almost a daily struggle with anguish over how to do things and serve the Lord . . . but thank God those days are over now."

I asked the Reverend Dennis Bennett, "Are you always a happy person?" He answered me candidly, "No, I'm not. I have been a minister for thirty-some years and have felt it was my duty to be happy even when I wasn't. Ministers *have* to be happy, I thought. I could very easily be like the fellow who says, 'Why pray when you can worry?' but I fight it. After thirty-some years I've learned I'm okay no matter how I feel. One of the things that has been the most meaningful to me has been counseling with my wife, Rita, for the healing of the inner souls of people.''

One of your best tools for attaining okayness is *giving*. When you reach out from yourself to help somebody else or to touch someone's life in a meaningful way, you conquer the grip negative feelings can clutch you with. Jess Moody said, ''God has not called us to see through each other but to see each other through.'' Dr. Alfred Adler said, ''It is the individual who is not interested in his fellow man who has the greatest difficulties in life and provides the greatest injuries to others.''

When we are feeling our most disturbed, as we discussed at the beginning of this chapter, is when we are the least giving. You can resist the urge to retreat into your hurts and feelings of inadequacies. You can fight those tendencies to avoid people and remain alone in your hurts. When I have hurt I have forced myself to give to someone else, even if the tears were still burning my cheeks. There's a saying I cherish and tell myself often: ''A bit of fragrance always clings to the hand that gives you roses.''

I decided a long time ago to be a rose giver. I believe we can all be rose givers in our unique ways, even if we feel we're worthless nothings and who would want a rose from us anyhow? I want the fragrance of my gifts around me. I want to be free to be giving and loving instead of entrapped in problems restricting me from the fragrance of roses. I tell myself, as you must, that I'm not the only person on earth who faces and must handle difficult problems.

## Your Problems Can Be an Advantage

When I think I am the only person who has a problem, I remember this favorite story of mine that Pope John XXIII told about himself. He admitted, ''It often happens that I wake at night and begin to think about a serious problem and decide I must tell the Pope about it. Then I wake up completely and remember that I *am* the Pope.''

At times we see our problems as so overwhelming that we lose sight of the truth that no problem is impossible to God. He always causes us to triumph. The Word tells us, ''Now thanks be unto God, which *always causeth us to triumph in Christ*, and maketh manifest the savour of his knowledge by us in every place'' (2 Corinthians 2:14, italics mine).

The following letter from a ''Dear Abby'' column in the *Los Angeles Times* challenges me when I think myself less than worthy. It was written to the Pastoral Relations Committee at a church by a prospective minister applying for the position of pastor:

*Gentlemen: Understanding your pulpit is vacant, I should like to apply for the position. I have many qualifications. . . . I've been a preacher with much success and also had some success as a writer. Some say I'm a good organizer. I've been a leader most places I've been.*

*I'm over fifty years of age. I have never preached in one place for more than three years. In some places I have left town after my work has caused riots and disturbances. I must admit I have been in jail three or four times, but not because of any real wrongdoing. My health is not good, though I still get a great deal done. The churches I have preached in have been small, though located in several large cities. I've not gotten along well with religious leaders in towns where I have preached. In fact, some have threatened me and even attacked me physically. I am not good at keeping records. I have been known to forget whom I have baptized. However, if you can use me, I shall do my best for you.*

You can imagine the response of the committee. The good church folks were aghast. They certainly did not want to call an unhealthy, troublemaking, absentminded, ex-jail bird up to see if he wanted the job. They couldn't believe anyone like that would have the nerve to apply for the position of minister for their little church. ''Who wrote that letter?'' asked a board member.

The board member, holding the letter, eyed them keenly and said, ''It's signed, 'The Apostle Paul.' ''

How often our efforts are misunderstood. How often we go unrecognized, unnoticed for heroic deeds. Dr. Robert Lewis, author of *Taking Chances*, wrote, ''For every Romeo who gains immortality for having lost his life and his Juliet, there are thousands of losers who go unsung.'' The price you pay for courage is suffering. I have remembered for a long time something said by William Faulkner. It moved me quite deeply the first time I heard it and it still does: ''If I were to choose between pain and nothing I would choose pain.'' No matter what our current experience is in life, we can make something beautiful out of it. It was David who wrote, "I will sing of the mercies of the Lord for ever: with my mouth will I make known thy faithfulness to all generations" (Psalms 89:1). The Apostle Paul wrote, "I have learned, in whatsoever state I am, therewith to be content" (Philippians 4:11). Such words are not spoken without the knowledge of pain.

## Discovering Your Personal Reality

Not long ago, I had a conversation in my living room with a delightful seventy-year-old lady. She was visiting us from out of town and I asked her what made her such a happy person. She told me, "You know, Marie, it's funny. When you get to be my age and you look back on the past you see how much time you wasted being concerned over things that really didn't matter at all. Here I am almost seventy years old and it really doesn't matter that my son left the bathroom light on when he was a child or that my husband came home late some evenings, or that I spent too much money on lettuce, or that apple juice was spilled on the carpet twenty-five years ago. I remember getting so excited and so upset over things that really were inconsequential in the total scheme of things. Now I know that what really matters is loving God with a pure heart and loving others with that same love."

Her eyes twinkled as she said, "It feels wonderful to be free now of all the silly, stupid things I was so concerned with for so many years. I no longer worry about who likes me or who doesn't." She chuckled and nudged my arm. "After all, I've read *your* books. It's really true that love covers a multitude of sins—but love is God and it's His Spirit that leads me now instead of my own will."

The Holy Spirit wants to lead you but He will never remove your own will so that you are powerless to choose. He leads us as we choose to walk in the power of the Holy Spirit, as Galatians 5:16 NAS says: "Walk by the Spirit, and you will not carry out the desire of the flesh." This means to be constantly guided and guarded by the Holy Spirit within us. The nearest thing to heaven is Jesus, and He lives in us by His Spirit. That means heaven is nearer than we think.

**Don't substitute your human spirit for the Holy Spirit.**

In the New Testament, the Greek word translated as ''flesh'' is *sarx,* and Paul uses this word ninety-one times in his letters. He tells us to make no provision for the flesh (Romans 13:14). We are not to feed this self-centered human nature. We are to feed our spirits with the power of the Holy Spirit in order to be conquerors of the defeating negative grip of a hostile devil and a hostile, unhappy world. We are to find our reality in Jesus. All else is meaningless.

## The Unhappy World Around You

One of my patients told me with great insight one day, ''Marie, I have a 'Conquer Complex.' '' She went on to tell me how she viewed most things in the world around her as a conflict to conquer. She rightly observed a world around her full of problems and troubled people. The problem is not so much the troubled world but what we do about it. Are we going to fall apart in discouragement, fear, and confusion over the fact that God has not stopped all wars and disease? My patient's biggest job of conquering was when she told me, ''I've stopped demanding 'why' of God. So there's sin and trouble and death. I can handle that and go on with my life as a person of faith.''

A valuable skill is to know what you can change and what you cannot. As a Christian you know your prayers can work miracles. One of the main differences between an adult and a child is the broader range of behaviors the adult has learned in order to cope with the problems, disappointments, and pressures of life. Too many times we think more about living tomorrow than we do about rejoicing today.

The most amazing thing happens when we decide to allow the Holy Spirit to make us happy in spite of whatever is going on around us. Thomas Jefferson wrote in a letter to Lafayette: ''We are not expected to be translated from despotism to liberty in a feather bed.'' It costs something to be a conqueror. You create victory with your Holy Spirit-empowered effort and true determination to conquer defeat.

One of my favorite artists, Louise Nevelson, said, "I have made my world and it's a much better world than I ever saw outside." The truly creative person, which you are because you have the Holy Spirit within you, is able to make something lovely out of something unlovely. You are able to make something joyful out of something sad. You are able to create something exciting out of something dull, something bright out of something dark, and something good out of something bad. By this creativity, inspired by God Himself, you change the world.

How do you describe your world? An American visited the Sudan, supposedly an underdeveloped country, and talked with that nation's president. The foreign president spoke of violence and drug abuse in America and concluded, "We feel that *you* come from a very undeveloped part of the world." What you tell yourself about your world is what you believe. Abraham Heschel, in his book of essays titled *The Insecurity of Freedom,* wrote, "Sanctity of life means that man is a partner, not a sovereign, that life is a trust, not a property." He said, "To be human is to celebrate a greatness which surpasses the self." He talks of the world we live in and concludes, "Some of us may find it difficult to believe that God created the world, yet most of us find it even more difficult to act as if man had not created the world."

The world you were born into is filled with negativity. God does not want you to run from negativity but to face it. *You* are not negative. Just as God's will was for Jesus to go to the cross and come through it, He wants you to come through your problems and struggles.

You struggle because you're trying to go somewhere. You have dreams and hopes and goals. They are important to you. Identify one major dream now. Name one goal.

Whenever you're trying to get somewhere with your life, the important thing is getting there. God wants you to arrive. He told His disciples to go to the other side. *Do what you are afraid to do.* Give where you are afraid to give. Negativity is *around* you, not *in* you.

## Your World Needs You

A twenty-four-year-old woman named Carmen recently had a liver transplant operation. Before the operation she didn't think she had a future. Everyone expected her to die of liver disease. Now, however, since the surgery was a success, she has a future. In an article in the *Los Angeles Times* she expressed that she didn't know what to do with her life now that she had one. Carmen no longer worried about dying, she worried about living. She told in the interview how she worried again about politics, crime, and nuclear war. Carmen has to learn how to live all over again. She said in the interview, "There are so many things out there I want to learn. I'd like to help people in some way. . . . I'd like to know that if someone's in trouble, I could help them . . . to be able to listen, to say something." With her new appreciation for life, it hurts Carmen to see it being abused.

Life needs you because the world needs God. The world lives with clenched fists. Your expression of God is very important to the world. Your hand reaching out to an unhappy world is vital. "You cannot shake hands with a clenched fist," said Indira Gandhi. You can open those fists.

I asked Dr. Lloyd Ogilve what he liked best about himself and he told me, "I like the fact that God has given me the ability to communicate with people. *I enjoy being able to communicate God's love to people.*" This busy minister takes time to pause and realize how much God loves him just as he is and then, as he told me, "I'm free to care for people as they are." Eleanor Roosevelt said, "The giving of love is an education in itself."

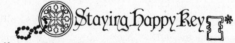

**Staying Happy Key I***

**Forgive the world and its unfairness. Love God even though you think He has disappointed you. Forgive the world and its unhappiness.**

You were created to love and to give. Rabbi Harold Cushner said, "The penalty for not being able to love imperfect people is condemning oneself to loneliness." If you are only success-oriented and not people-oriented, the road to success can dehumanize you. You may repress emotions, limit your recreation, and eliminate friendships. It's important to have single-minded determination in your work because what you love the most you will grow to resemble.

## Letting Go

How many times have you ever longed to be tense and unhappy? Have you ever longed to be paralyzed by anxiety and irrational fears? When was the last time you planned to experience high blood pressure, headaches, and a lower energy level? Now let me ask you, do you plan for letting go of tension? Take time every day to plan how *not* to be stressful. Make lists of things to do, such as the following, to keep yourself in a peaceful and happy state:

### "I Release" Exercise

1. Sit in a comfortable chair. Allow yourself to relax as you breathe slowly and evenly.
2. As you exhale, say "I release," and as you do, allow the tension, negative thoughts, and painful feelings to be released. Imagine these things leaving you.
3. Repeat over and over again "I release" and name what you release. Experience the tension leaving your body as you release willingly.
4. Now fill yourself with peaceful, happy thoughts. Replace the tension with sweetness and peace.

## Where Does Stress Belong in Your Life?

Research shows that intensity of stress is not as damaging as the duration of stress can be. The more continual the stress, the more energy is required to cope with it. When you are continually stressed, you experience a continual loss of energy. This is called *distress*. Most of us are familiar with this condition. *Eustress*, on the other hand, is when there is enough time to adapt to reenergize.

Stress is due to conflict and change. Not all stress is bad. Stress is often a motivator causing you to take positive action. Sometimes we think work in itself is stressful. Not true. Work may be the best thing in the world for you. Hans Selye, in his book *Stress Without Distress*, says, "Do not listen to the tempting slogans of those who keep repeating, 'There is more to life than just work,' or 'You should work to live, not live to work.' " Dr. Selye claims, quite convincingly, that our principal aim should not be to avoid work and stress but to find the kind of occupation and activities which, for us, are play.

I have noticed in my own life that what for me is challenging and exciting would be quite terrifying for another person. I find it joyous and exciting to write books, travel, speak for God, and teach. My secretary, on the other hand, finds standing in front of a group of people quite stressful. She loves her work running the office and tending to the many administrative details of her job. I would find that quite stressful.

You can employ and practice stress-reduction exercises such as the ones I have shared with you, but it is also important to listen to the messages you give yourself about your daily life. Your principal aim must never be to avoid work but to avoid the harmful stress of work. Select friends and people to surround you who are blessings. Your activities should be ones you truly enjoy. The way to eliminate stress is to plan your relationships and activities according to your personality and likes. Constant need for release, adapting, and energy to cope is wearing.

One of the major sources of distress is dissatisfaction with your life and your accomplishments. This can be positive in that it may motivate you to make some changes. Stress in the body is also the mobilization of its defenses to allow you to adapt to events that are hostile or threatening. Stress is associated with pleasant and unpleasant experiences, and the only time you will be without it completely is when you are dead. Since we can't avoid stress, we can learn how to meet it effectively and actually enjoy it.

As you analyze your life and your behaviors, you can develop your own personal recovery plan and Staying Happy plan. The causes of unhappiness, excessive stress, and frustration are found in the three A's:

1. Excessive need for Approval
2. Excessive need for Attention
3. Excessive need for Appreciation

*Need for Approval.* This need causes you to be supersensitive to anything less than total achievement and approval. You may be depressed at any lack of appreciation or any form of rejection that comes your way. In order to live with a maximum of joy and satisfaction in your life, with a minimum of needless pain and dissatisfaction, you must learn to interpret your stressors. Counteract that misbelief of needing the approval of one and all. It is not imperative. (Reread chapter 7.)

*Need for Attention.* You deserve attention. A problem arises when it is not immediate. When you are giving and loving and self-sacrificing, you may feel that if you are not rewarded with attention and praise you are being rejected or somehow abused. Your yearning for rewards and attention becomes compulsive when you work constantly doing good things to get attention, appreciation, and credit. You will feel deprived when attention is not paid. This is quite stressful and it is important to examine your motives in your self-sacrificing behavior. If you are a parent, it can be particularly stressful to give so much of your heart and soul if there is not some gratifying reward on the immediate horizon.

*Need for Appreciation.* The need for appreciation is closely related to the need for attention. These needs in themselves are healthy and realistic. The danger point is in *excessiveness*. I have emphasized the need for a feeling of competence. If you will tell yourself the truth, which is that you have the ability and the wherewithal within you to perform competently and effectively in those things which you choose to do, your sense of hunger for appreciation will diminish. You are your strongest rewarder. You are your primary and best friend, next to the Lord Jesus. You are gifted to appreciate yourself and to bestow yourself with words of respectful admiration. What you value should be your own opinion. If others do not give you appreciation for your efforts, you must not be left feeling bereft and rejected. Your attitudes and your opinions of what you do and who you are are more important. A favorable impression of yourself will alleviate your desperate need for the appreciation of others.

In your drive for approval, attention, and appreciation, you will find constant frustration, which is a constant stress. The root of your stress, I must repeat, is the value and meaning you assign to things. How you respond to a particular event is determined solely by your attitudes. You can actually turn negative stress into a positive experience. Since you have the mind of Christ and that same Spirit which raised Him from the dead dwells in you, you have the ability to turn bad to good. Even when your schedule is jammed with too much work and there are pressures and demands coming at you from all sides, you can creatively respond instead of giving way to stress and distress.

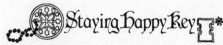

**Take the loving, appreciating, and rewarding attitudes of Jesus as your own.**

## I Believe I'm Good Enough

*Marie, I actually joined that singles group we talked about. I forced myself to go to the meeting the third time, and though I dreaded it because I thought it would be a lonely and alienating experience, I went anyway. You had told me that if I continued to feed myself such negative self-talk and if I continued to believe such depressing things, I would rob myself of a lot of happiness. Well, I knew what you were telling me was true, but I had formed such a negative habit of believing in doom that it was hard to change. Then you told me even if things went well for me when I forced myself to do things I didn't want to, I could still be hurting myself. You insisted that I tell myself words I thought Jesus would be telling me. That made me really think. It shocked me when I discovered that my impression of Jesus was really shameful. I had never really thought of Him talking sweetly or nicely to me. I never realized it, but my version of Jesus was of a cruel and heartless master. You forced me to see Him as loving and kind.*

*I could have gone to the singles group and been blessed as I was, even though I complained all the way there. You wouldn't settle for that. You insisted I conquer the complaining. Well, I did. You know how hard it was for me because you stood with me through it all, but Marie, I am free. I actually know and believe in the heart of me I am somebody. I honestly believe I am good enough now. You always told me I was never good enough because of what I am or do but because of who Jesus Christ is within me. How can I tell you the happiness I feel because I understand now!*

*I believe I can do things. I can accomplish things. I can make good things happen because of the creative power of God within me—I am a child of God! How can I thank you for showing me the way? Yes, I joined the singles group. It was the breaking of my self-will for me. It was more than just moving outside of myself to make social improvements. When I went to that group with an expectant heart and a mind that was free and actually looking forward to giving as well as receiving, as we talked about, it was as though the chains of my confined and painful past fell from me. I know I can do all things through Christ who strengtheneth me. Those are no longer just words other people say and believe. I believe now, too! I have made many new friends because you forced me to take steps to change my life. Not only have I made friends but I have changed jobs and I'm even planning on making a move to live in a place where I will be happier. I am anxious to talk to you about all of these things and share with you more of what God has done. I am thrilled finally to find the real me and to discover I like me!*

## The Staying Happy Recovery Plan

The above letter emphasizes how exciting it is to discover oneself. The journey we are taking together in this book is probably the most important journey of our lives. This time together is a time for self-discovery, and whereas other books may tell you how to change the world, this one guides you in how to change yourself. When you are entering your Staying Happy recovery plan, you are something like a starfish, one of the most amazing of God's creations. A starfish simply curls one of its five points when it wants to go somewhere and it can move in any direction without turning. A most clever creation, and wonderful because if it loses something of itself, it can actually regenerate that something. Possibly you have experienced loss in your life, as I have. *You can regenerate.*

Perhaps you, too, have hurt and felt there was nowhere to turn. Perhaps you wrestle with stress and pressure daily, along with feelings of inadequacy and fear of the future. Perhaps you feel unlovable and left out of the mainstream of life.

Discover yourself and what makes you so unique. Self-discovery releases the trap of your own self-defenses. Hurt, fear of rejection, and all of the other dreads that have gripped you with fear can be confronted because once you learn your Staying Happy principles and live them, you will discover God in a new way. Not that He says you'll never hurt again, but He is *with* you and *in* you through all things. Your value can't be squashed out, even in the face of adversity. Love can't be burned or flooded or stolen from you because no sorrow, trial, or misery can take it from you. I don't appreciate pep talks when I'm hurting, so I imagine you don't, either. In that case, here's the truth: You and God are one. He loves you. You're valuable. You can handle trial and pain.

I spoke at a women's retreat in San Francisco recently and an energetic and vibrant elderly woman came up to me and asked me to pray that God would give her a ministry in her church. I looked at her radiant face, lined with years, and I asked her, "When you are unhappy, how does Jesus help you regain your happiness?" She thought for the briefest moment and then said, with her eyes twinkling, "Marie, I can't say I ever get unhappy."

"You're *never* unhappy?"

"No, I'm not. Not anymore."

"Then you already have your ministry," I said resolutely, and I prayed for the countless souls she would lead into the kingdom. A happy heart is everyone's medicine and our world is hurting for such a healing.

Your possibilities are unending. I pray one day you'll say, like the woman, "I can't say I ever get unhappy." She confirmed something very important to me that day: we were born again in Christ to be happy and stay happy, no matter how unhappy our world is or how unhappy the situation around us may be.

## Staying Happy Gifts

This list of ten Staying Happy gifts to yourself are your personal commitments to yourself. I've adapted them from Dale Carnegie and I share them with you because they work. If you will follow these ten points you can discover the freedom and happiness you deserve and long for. No matter how giving or loving you may think you already are, you can still grow to greater depths of God's ability. You can still learn more about the joy of the Lord.

The following list is a *daily* commitment.

1. Today I will be happy. I will be happy with myself, my work, and my endeavors. I will be happy with what I have and where I am.

2. Today I will not try to change the world to fit my demands and expectations. I will be at peace with the world and the people around me.

3. Today I will bless my body by exercising, eating nutritiously, and declining the temptation to neglect my health.

4. Today I will discover something new and interesting. I will do this by studying, reading, observing, and listening. I will record on paper at least one new thing that I discover and learn today.

5. Today I will do something good for somebody else without their knowing it was me who did it. I will be a channel of blessing for someone today because I am a giver.

6. Today I will look as good as I can. I will dress becomingly, groom myself carefully, and wear a pleasing expression on my face.

7. Today I will not find fault or criticize one person, and I will not try to improve anyone's behavior.

8. Today I will live this day alone and not try to conquer all of life at once.

9. Today I will make a plan for my activities. I will schedule my hours and not allow my enemies, Rush and Indecision, to overwhelm my precious time.

10. Today I will give myself the right to make mistakes, to be imperfect and still feel good. Today I believe I am worthy of being loved.

I *can* stay happy in an unhappy world.

To order the three-cassette tape album of Marie Chapian teaching *Staying Happy in an Unhappy World* and additional words of help and encouragement, write to:

Marie Chapian Ministries
P.O. Box 16655
San Diego, CA 92116

## SELF-DISCOVERY QUESTIONNAIRE

Your age _____

Occupation _____

Male ____ Female ____

U.S. Citizen _____ Other _____

Health ____  Good ____  Fair ____  Bad

1. What I like best about myself is: _____
2. What I like least about myself is: _____
3. I am a person who _____
4. When are you the happiest? _____
5. When in your past were you the happiest? _____
6. How much of the time during an ordinary week do you feel truly happy?
   Always_____ Sometimes _____ Never _____
7. Do you enjoy children? Enormously_____ A lot_____
   Tolerate them_____ Not at all_____
8. What in your opinion is "success"? _____
9. Do you enjoy the work you do? _____
10. What best applies to your work situation? (Check as many as apply.)
    I hate it. ____ I'm trapped in a situation I can't get out of.____
    It pays good money so I stay. _____ It pays poorly but I love it.____ I am where I have worked hard to be. _____ I have attained my goal. ____ I am challenged and motivated in my work.

    _____
11. How do you get along with those who have authority over you?
    Very well _____ Tolerably _____ Resentfully _____
12. Do you have a best friend with whom you can share your deepest feelings and thoughts? _____
13. Would you rather work alone or with others when getting an important job done? _____
14. Have you ever felt you're going crazy? _____
15. What do you think is the greatest achievement you have made in your life? _____
16. What is your worst failure? _____
17. How many vacations do you take a year? _____ How long?

    _____

18. Do you go away from home on vacations? _____

19. When you have a task ahead of you that you don't like or want to do, what do you do? Put it off till tomorrow. _____ Do it immediately to get it out of the way. _____

20. If you were at work and had to decide whether to complete a tedious, difficult task or not, would you: Work overtime to get the job done. _____ Go home because you don't get paid for overtime. _____

21. How often do you attend church? Every Sunday _____ Twice a month _____ Less than twice a month _____

22. Are you active in a prayer group or fellowship that meets during the week? _____

23. Have you ever had a private meal with your pastor and his family? _____

24. Does your pastor know you by name? _____

25. Have you set goals for your career? _____

26. Have you set goals for your personal life? _____

27. Does someone else or something else determine your goals for you? _____ Explain: _____

28. Are you content with your current home? _____
Explain: _____

29. What do you do to feel better when you're depressed? _____
_____

30. How do you handle stress? _____

31. If you were to change anything in your life, what would it be?
_____

32. If you could be anyone in the world, who would it be? _____

33. If you could have any job or position in the world, what would it be? _____
_____

34. Complete: One of the things I feel guilty about is: _____
One of the ways people hurt me is: _____
If I weren't afraid to be myself, I would: _____

35. List the qualities that, in your opinion, make a person heroic or great. _____
_____

# BIBLIOGRAPHY

Allen, Charles L. *The Touch of the Master's Hand*. Old Tappan, New Jersey: Fleming H. Revell Company, 1966.

Arieti, Silvano. *Creativity: The Magic Synthesis*. New York: Basic Books, 1976.

Bowls, Richard Nelson. *What Color Is Your Parachute?* Ten Speed Press, 1983.

Bosworth, F. F. *Christ the Healer*. Old Tappan, New Jersey: Fleming H. Revell Company, 1973.

Burns, David, M.D. *Feeling Good: The New Mood Therapy*. New American Library, 1981.

Chapian, Marie. *Escape From Rage*. New Jersey: Bridge Publishers, 1981.

————. *Love and Be Loved*. Old Tappan, New Jersey: Fleming H. Revell Company, 1983.

————. *Of Whom the World Was Not Worthy*. Minneapolis, Minnesota: Bethany House Publishers, 1978.

Chapian, Marie, and Backus, William, M.D. *Telling Yourself the Truth*. Minneapolis, Minnesota: Bethany House Publishers, 1980.

*Diagnostic and Statistical Manual of Mental Disorders,* Third Edition. Washington D.C.: American Psychiatric Association, 1968.

Fromm, Erich. *The Art of Loving*. New York: Harper and Row, 1956.

Harris, Thomas. *I'm OK–You're OK*. New York: Harper and Row, 1967.

Horney, Karen. *The Neurotic Personality of Our Time*. New York: W. W. Norton and Co., 1950.

Lehner, George, and Kube, Ella. *The Dynamics of Personal Adjustment*. Englewood Cliffs, New Jersey: Prentice-Hall, Inc., 1955.

Maslow, Abraham H. "Deprivation, Threat and Frustration." *Psychological Review,* vol. 48, 1941.

Naisbitt, John. *Megatrends*. New York: Warner Books, 1984.

Osborn, Alex. *Applied Imagination*. New York: Scribners, 1953.

Pfeiffer, Karl, M.D., Ph.D. *Mental and Elemental Nutrients*. New Canaan, Connecticut: Keats Publishing, Inc., 1975.

Satir, Virginia. *Self-Esteem*. Millbrae, California: Celestial Arts, 1970.

Selye, Hans. *Stress Without Distress*. New York: Harper and Row, 1974.

Tavris, Carol. *Anger: The Misunderstood Emotion*. New York: Simon & Schuster, 1982.

Torrance, E. P. *Guiding Creative Talent*. Englewood Cliffs, New Jersey: Prentice-Hall, Inc., 1962.

Trobisch, Walter. *Love Yourself*. Downers Grove, Illinois: Inter-Varsity Press, 1976.

Waitley, Denis. *Seeds of Greatness*. Old Tappan, New Jersey: Fleming H. Revell Company, 1983.

Wood, John T. *What Are You Afraid Of?* Englewood Cliffs, New Jersey: Prentice-Hall, Inc., 1976.